Linguistically and Culturally Diverse Students

Cooperative Educational Service Agency No. 9
Milwaukee Public Schools
Wisconsin Department of Public Instruction

Christine Freiberg
Speech and Language Pathologist
Wausau School District
Content Coordinator

Department of Public Instruction
Madison, Wisconsin

This publication is available from
Publication Sales
Wisconsin Department of Public Instruction
Drawer 179
Milwaukee, WI 53293-0179
(800) 243-8782

This publication was developed under an Individuals with Disabilities Education Act (IDEA) discretionary grant in cooperation with Milwaukee Public Schools and Cooperative Educational Service Agency (CESA) 9, administered by the Department of Public Instruction, Division for Learning Support: Equity & Advocacy.

Bulletin No. 98148

ISBN 1-57337-049-5

Printed on recycled paper.

Table of Contents

Foreward

Wisconsin has long been a leader in the field of education. In an effort to sustain that leadership, educators have recognized that the state must be diligent in their efforts to continually monitor assessment and evaluation methods as well as intervention strategies for students in the area of general and special education. In an effort to address some of these issues, a statewide task force was established to develop guidance in the assessment procedures of African American and Hmong students who are experiencing academic and communication difficulties in the educational environment. It is anticipated that the information in this guide will provide guidance to speech and language pathologists and others who are responsible for assessment of students from these target populations.

The guide provides information pertaining to:
- cultural factors influencing learning and language;
- recommended procedures for complete and appropriate non-biased assessment;
- data collected as a result of analysis of language samples of typically developing Hmong and African American children;
- dialectical and phonological patterns that should not be considered errors;
- some intervention strategies for regular education teachers; and
- case studies.

Although this guide specifically addresses children who are African American or Hmong, educators in both general and special education will find the information useful in their work with students from other bilingual and cultural groups. It is my pleasure to offer this publication, *Linguistically Culturally Diverse*, to achieve such purpose.

John T. Benson
State Superintendent

Acknowledgments

The Wisconsin Department of Public Instruction (DPI), Milwaukee Public Schools (MPS), and Cooperative Educational Service Agency (CESA) 9 gratefully acknowledge the contributions of these dedicated people who have given their valuable time and expertise to the development of this publication. All of the following contributors are speech and language pathologists (SLPs) except William Xiong, who is a school counselor. A special thanks to Barbara Leadholm, education consultant, Speech and Language Program, for the DPI until 1995, for her support in the development of the grant that led to this guide and for her continued interest in this project. Thanks also to the school districts and university communicative disorder departments for allowing their staff members to participate in the creation of this guide.

Nancy Almandinger
Wausau School District

Marsha Blake-Gayfield
Milwaukee Public Schools

Eleanor Brush
University of Wisconsin-Stevens Point

Mila Ong Caceres
Milwaukee Public Schools

Linda Carpenter
University of Wisconsin-Eau Claire

Mary Garves
La Crosse School District

Audrey C. George
Milwaukee Public Schools

Marianne Gill
Madison Metropolitan School District

Ann Gorton
Eau Claire School District

Kathleen Lyngaas
Madison Metropolitan School District

Jon F. Miller
University of Wisconsin-Madison

Jan Molaska
Wausau School District

Sue Retzlaff
La Crosse School District

Carol Schmidt
Milwaukee Public Schools

Joan Suick
Eau Claire School District

Paul H. Thielhelm
Sheboygan School District

William Xiong
Milwaukee Public Schools

A special thank you to the two project directors: David Damgaard, special education/pupil services director for the Wausau School District, and James Larson, regional services coordinator for CESA 9, Tomahawk, Wisconsin. The following individuals, listed by the agency they represent, also contributed to the overall success of the project.

Department of Public Instruction

John T. Benson
State Superintendent

Juanita Pawlisch
Administrator, Division for Learning Support:
    Equity and Advocacy

Paul Halverson,
Director, Division for Learning Support:
    Equity and Advocacy

Brent Odell
School Administration Consultant

Kate Morand
Education Consultant
    Speech and Language Program

Milwaukee Public Schools

Tamara Cornelius
Speech and Language Pathologist

Sharon Dye
Speech and Language Pathologist

Denise Morris
Speech and Language Pathologist

Audrey Potter
Federal Programs, Department of Special
    Education and Supportive Services

Wanda Richards-Miller
Speech and Language Pathologist

Jacqueline Servi Margis
English as a Second Language Curriculum
    Specialist

Frances Smith
Speech and Language Pathologist

Robert Sullivan
Federal Programs, Department of Special
    Educationand Supportive Services

Ge Xiong
Southeast Asian Parent Liaison

Wausau School District

Lynell Anderson
ESL Program Director

Mary Ellen Marnholtz
PR/Communication Director
    (cover design)

Nancy Puetz
Educational Audiologist

Peter Yang
Director
    Wausau Hmong Association

Thank you also to the State Superintendent's Advisory Council on Bilingual/ESL Education; Harriette Smith, administrative assistant, CESA 9; Choua Lo, interpreter/translator, La Crosse School District; Victor Xiong, Hmong community leader, Milwaukee; and Diane Scott and Karen Beverly-Ducker, American Speech and Hearing Association Multicultural Affairs Department, Rockville, Maryland.

1

Perspectives: Ethical, Historical, Legal, and Demographic

Introduction

For several decades, speech and language pathologists (SLPs) have attempted to determine how best to provide services for children whose native language is not English or to children who speak different dialects of American English. The central challenge facing speech and language pathologists who deal with students from linguistically and culturally diverse (LCD) backgrounds is distinguishing communication differences related to linguistic or cultural factors from communication disorders. This is first and foremost an ethical and legal responsibility. History provides an opportunity to see why this distinction is so important and how these ethical and legal responsibilities evolved.

From a historical perspective, the civil rights movement of the 1960s marked the first time the United States recognized the needs of minority groups. In 1954, the U.S. Supreme Court ruled in Brown v. Board of Education that segregated education based on race was unequal and unconstitutional. This court ruling set the context for dealing with educational diversity issues. Since then, additional congressional, judicial, and executive actions on behalf of people of color, ethnic minorities, and individuals with disabilities have occurred.

Congressional Actions

Title VI of the Civil Rights Act of 1964
- Bilingual Education Acts of 1968, 1974, and 1979
- Section 504 of the Rehabilitation Act of 1973
- Equal Education Opportunity Act of 1974
- Individuals with Disabilities Education Act (IDEA), formerly the Education of All Handicapped Children Act of 1975
- Elementary and Secondary Education Act Amendment of 1978 (PL95-561)
- Amendments to the Bilingual Education Act, Title VII (PL98-511, 1984)
- Education of All Handicapped Children's Act Amendment of 1986 (PL 99-457)
- Americans with Disabilities Act (1992)
  These acts
—prohibited discrimination on the basis of race, color, national origin, handicap, or language;
—established due process rights for children and their parents;
—ensured students with disabilities who also are limited-English proficient (LEP) their right to access a "free appropriate public education;" and
—mandated non-discriminatory assessment.

Judicial Actions

- Arreola v. Board of Education (California, 1968)
- Lau v. Nichols (California, 1974)
- Diana v. The State Board of Education (California, 1970)
- Guadalupe v. Tempe Elementary School District (California, 1972)
- Lora v. Board of Education of the City of New York (New York, 1977)
- Larry P. v. Riles, Superintendent of Public Instruction for the State of California (California, 1979)
- Jose P. et al. v. Ambach et al. (New York City, 1979)
- Martin Luther King, Jr. Elementary School Children et al. v. Ann Arbor School Board (Michigan, 1979)

These right-to-education lawsuits were similar in that they
—were argued on the basis of biased assessments that led to disproportionate numbers of minorities in special education classes, and
—found standardized testing procedures to be racially, culturally, and linguistically discriminatory when test results were used to make special education placements.

Executive Actions

- U.S. Department of Health, Education, and Welfare Policy Guideline "Identification of Discrimination" (1979)
- Lau Remedies issued by the Office for Civil Rights (1975)
- U.S. Code of Federal Regulations, Number 34, Part 300.532 (a) (1973)
- PI 11 of the Wisconsin Administrative Code
- Wisconsin Department of Public Instruction publication *Parent and Child Rights in Special Education*, 1993

These executive actions
—provide direction to educational agencies and parents, and
—clarify the legal rights of individuals with disabilities and persons who are linguistically and culturally diverse.

About the same time these laws were adopted and court decisions were issued, an important event occurred within the profession of speech pathology and audiology. In 1968, at the annual convention of the American Speech and Hearing Association (ASHA), Orlando Taylor of Indiana University and John Michel of the University of Kansas debated "The Role of a Professional Association in a Conflict Society." Michel took the position that professional associations should not become involved in social issues, while Taylor took the opposite position. The debate stimulated much discussion within the speech and language profession, and some members formed a Black Caucus within ASHA. Prior to 1968, there was little professional literature that dealt with the issue of distinguishing language and speech **differences** from true language and speech **disorders**. In 1969, the Black Caucus issued a report that enunciated the need to do so. The Black Caucus wrote:

"Unfortunately, far too many speech pathologists view legitimate language differences among Afro-Americans from a pathology model. The result is that a number of black children are receiving speech and language therapy, particularly in urban areas, when they, in fact, have no pathology. Negative psychological effects on the black child are obvious. In order to develop a more intelligent approach to recognizing legitimate linguistic differences and satisfactory methods for second language instruction as a skill, clinicians need training in sociolinguistics (interaction between language and culture) and the historical and cultural roots of black children. All too often clinicians fail to understand the black child's language, as well as the child himself. ... Unless the profession of communication disorders begins to put forth a major thrust in this area, it will lose a great opportunity to catapult itself into an arena of great educational and cultural interest" (Taylor, 1986, p. 5).

Numerous important actions have occurred within the speech and language pathology profession in response to the concerns and issues raised by the Black Caucus. The following events occurred in response to the Michel-Taylor debate and the advocacy of the ASHA Black Caucus.

- ASHA established several offices and committees (for example, Office of Minority Concerns, Committee on Cultural and Linguistic Differences and Disorders of Communication, and Committee on the Status of Racial Minorities).

• ASHA issued position statements on social dialects and clinical management of communicatively minority language populations. Essentially, it is ASHA's position that the speech and language pathologist must make a distinction between communication differences and communication disorders. ASHA's position is that ethically "once the difference/disorder distinctions have been made, it is the role of the SLP to treat only those features or characteristics that are true errors and not those attributable to the dialect" (ASHA, September 1983, p. 24).

• Universities established special training programs and projects to address the unique needs of linguistically and culturally diverse populations.

• Presentations at professional meetings and reports in professional journals on topics related to linguistic and cultural diversity increased dramatically (Taylor, 1986, pp. 3-5).

Simultaneously, other professional groups and individuals were focusing attention on language rights as civil rights, not just for African American students but also for Hispanic, Asian, and Native American students. It became apparent that discriminatory assessment procedures were violating the civil rights of students, and biased assessment practices led to inappropriate classifications and placements.

In 1968, L.M. Dunn, who developed the Peabody Picture Vocabulary Text, first identified the problem of disproportionately high placements of racial minority students in special education programs. Five years later, J.R. Mercer published a report on her study of special education placements which confirmed that LCD students were being misidentified as students with special education needs. Early reports indicated an overrepresentation of African American and Hispanic American students in special education, particularly in classes for students with mental retardation (Mercer, 1973).

Recent reports have shown some shifts in numbers, yet disproportionately high numbers of African American, Native American, and Hispanic American students are placed in special education programs for students with mild disabilities. Asian Americans, on the other hand, tend to be underrepresented in special education programs (Harry, 1992, p. 66).

Placement figures by race and disability vary from state to state and from school district to school district. In addition, studies have shown that placement patterns have changed somewhat over time. For example, the disproportionately high number of students from minority populations in classes for students with cognitive disabilities (CD) has been somewhat resolved; however, it has been replaced by disproportionately large numbers of minorities in programs for students with learning disabilities (LD). More recently, this disproportionate number of LD placements has given way to speech and language placements as school districts have sought less restrictive exceptional education placements (Carpenter, 1990, pp. 70-71).

Nationally, as well as in Wisconsin, concern that the diagnosis of a speech and/or language disability is applied to students who display language or cultural differences and not true disorders is growing. Studies conducted in Texas and California have shown that special education processes continue to be problematic for Hispanic American students. Figure 1 summarizes the findings of two research institutes and illustrates the nature of the problems still confronting the SLP profession nearly two decades after the legal mandates for non-discriminatory special education practices.

Figure 1

Summary of Findings from the Texas and California Handicapped Minority Research Institutes

(Reprinted with permission from "Bilingual Special Education and This Special Issue" by R.A. Figueroa, S.H. Fradd, and V.I. Correa. *Exceptional Chlidren*, October 1989, pp. 174-178.)

Assessment

- Language proficiency is not seriously taken into account in special education.
- Testing is done primarily in English, often increasing the likelihood of establishing achievement or intelligence discrepancy.
- English language problems that are typically characteristic of second-language learners (poor comprehension, limited vocabulary, grammar and syntax errors, and problems with English articulation) are misinterpreted as handicaps.
- Learning disability and communication handicapped placements have replaced the misplacement of students as educable mentally retarded of the 1960s and 1970s.
- Psychometric test scores from Spanish or English tests are capricious in their outcomes, though, paradoxically, internally sound.
- Special education placement leads to decreased test scores (IQ and achievement).
- The same few tests are used with most children.
- Having parents born out of the United States increases the likelihood of being found eligible for special education.
- Re-evaluation usually led to more special education.

Intervention

- The behaviors that trigger teacher referral suggest that language-acquisition stages and their interaction with English-only programs are being confused for handicapped conditions.
- Few children receive primary language support before special education, even fewer, during special education.
- The second and third grades are critical for bilingual children in terms of potentially being referred.
- Pre-referral modifications of the regular programs are rare and show little indications of primary language support.
- Special education produced little academic development.
- Individual education plans had few, if any, accommodations for bilingual children.
- The few special education classes that work for children who are bilingual are more like good regular bilingual education classes (whole-language emphasis, comprehensible input, cooperative learning, and student empowerment) than traditional behavioristic, task-analysis driven, worksheets-oriented special education classes.

The authors who conducted this research found that many school districts were not adequately fulfilling their legal responsibilities for assessing a child in his or her native language. They further concluded that the total process of identification, referral, and assessment is loaded against the student with limited-English proficiency. Although this research was conducted on Hispanic American students, similar results are emerging in literature on Asian Americans and Native Americans. Students who are limited-English speaking or non-English speaking obviously present a challenge to school districts and in particular the assessment teams that often include the speech and language pathologist. Less obvious is the assessment challenge presented by African American students who speak a dialect of English.

Demographics provide a feeling for the scope and magnitude of what this means to school districts and their speech and language pathologists. According to 1990 census figures, approximately 26 percent of the U.S. population is nonwhite, and the number and proportion of minorities in this country is anticipated to increase. Another census projection suggests that sometime during the twenty-first century, the proportion of racial and ethnic minorities in U.S. schools will be greater than 50 percent (Cole and Deal, 1990).

Obviously, the numbers and percentages of students from linguistically and culturally diverse backgrounds in any given state or school district vary. While Wisconsin is not among the states with the highest numbers or percentages of its school-age population from linguistically and culturally diverse backgrounds, the challenge to an SLP who is asked to evaluate a student is nonetheless significant because

• few practicing SLPs have had university coursework to prepare them. According to a national survey conducted by C.A. Roseberry-McKibbin and G.E. Eicholtz in 1994, 65 percent of the SLPs surveyed reported that they had received no training pertinent to multicultural populations during their education programs. While this has improved in recent years, it remains a problem.

• few standardized, norm-referenced speech and language tests designed specifically for students from linguistically and culturally diverse backgrounds exist. Comments made ten years ago by experts in the field of speech pathology still hold true today.

"At present, there are no standardized assessment procedures that provide a valid evaluation of language disorders in speakers whose native language is not standard English" (Taylor, Payne, and Anderson, 1983)

"Given the present state of the art in speech and language tests, it can be concluded that there are few, if any, standardized measures that can provide a completely valid and non-biased evaluation of handicapping conditions for linguistically and culturally diverse populations" (Taylor and Payne, 1983).

"It is not an overstatement to say that a crisis exists in the area of assessment of non-mainstream speakers. ... Diagnosticians ... need valid, reliable assessment tools" (Vaughn-Cooke, 1983).

• few certified speech and language pathologists are fluent in a language other than English; and even fewer SLPs are members of, or completely sensitive to, cultures other than Eurocentric culture.

• major informational gaps exist in the literature concerning normal language development in non-Anglo populations. For example, only a few studies address normal development of African American English as a first language. No studies regarding acquisition of Hmong as a first language are available.

• few SLPs are aware of an inherent bias against students who are from linguistically and culturally diverse backgrounds.

• many SLPs lack knowledge regarding linguistic and cultural diversity.

• speech and language pathologists have an ethical responsibility to conform to the position statement of the American Speech-Language-Hearing Association (formerly the American Speech and Hearing Association) that "no dialectal variety of English is a disorder or a pathological form of speech or language. ... (However,) it is indeed possible for dialect speakers to have linguistic disorders within the dialect. An essential step toward making accurate assessments of communicative disorders is to distinguish between those aspects of linguistic variation that represent the diversity of the English language from those that represent speech, language, and hearing disorders" (ASHA, 1983).

• speech and language pathologists have a legal responsibility to conform to Wisconsin Administrative Code PI 11, which states that "educational needs resulting primarily from poverty; neglect; delinquency; social maladjustment; cultural or linguistic isolation; or inappropriate instruction are not included under subch. V., ch. 115, Stats."

• professionals who work with students who are linguistically and culturally diverse are required to possess certain competencies. ASHA standards indicate that professionals should have knowledge and proficiency in the student's language and home culture in order to work effectively with a student who is linguistically and culturally diverse.

Many speech and language professionals are well aware of their limitations when it comes to proficiency in a language other than English. They are also aware of their limited knowledge of diverse cultures. Such limitations restrict services for students who are linguistically and culturally diverse. Speech and language professionals are also keenly aware of their legal and ethical obligations to provide nonbiased assessments to determine if learning difficulties are due to language differences or a language disorder.

Given the challenges and limitations confronting SLPs as they prepare to deliver services to students who are linguistically and culturally diverse, it is imperative that they consider the factors that influence language acquisition and learning.

References

Ambert, Alba, and Nancy Dew. *Special Education for Exceptional Bilingual Students: A Handbook for Educators*. Milwaukee, WI: Midwest National Origin Desegregation Assistance Center, 1982.

American Speech-Language-Hearing Association. "Position Paper on Social Dialects." *ASHA*, September 1983.

American Speech-Language-Hearing Association. "Position Paper on Clinical Management of Communicatively Handicapped Minority Language Populations." *ASHA*, June 1985.

Baca, Leonard, and Jim Bransford. *An Appropriate Education for Handicapped Children of Limited English Proficiency*. Reston, VA: ERIC Clearinghouse, 1982.

Bergin, Victoria. *Special Education Needs in Bilingual Programs*. Rosslyn, VA: National Clearinghouse for Bilingual Education, 1980.

Carpenter, L.J. *Including Multicultural Content in the Undergraduate Communication Disorders Curriculum: A Resource Guide and Reference Document*. Eau Claire, WI: University of Wisconsin-Eau Claire, 1990.

Cole, Lorraine, and Vicki R. Deal. *100 Amazing Facts about Minorities and Communication Disorders*. ASHA Teleconference, May 25, 1990.

Damico, Jack S., and Else V. Hamayan. *Multicultural Language Intervention: Addressing Cultural and Linguistic Diversity*. Buffalo, NY: Educom Associates, Inc., 1992.

Dunn, L.M. "Special Education for Mildly Retarded—Is Much of it Justifiable?" *Exceptional Children* 35 (1968), pp. 5-21.

Figueroa, R.A., S.H. Fradd, and V.I. Correa. "Bilingual Special Education and This Special Issue." *Exceptional Children*, October 1989, pp 174-178.

Hamayan Else V., and Jack S. Damico. *Limiting Bias in the Assessment of Bilingual Students*: Austin, TX: Pro-ed, 1991.

Harry, Beth. *Cultural Diversity, Families, and the Special Education System*. Austin, TX: Pro-ed, 1992.

Langdon, Henriette W., with Li-Rong Lilly Cheng. *Hispanic Children and Adults with Communication Disorders: Assessment and Intervention*. Gaithersburg, MD: Aspen Publishers, Inc., 1992.

Mercer, J.R. *Labeling the Mentally Retarded: Clinical and Social System Perspective on Mental Retardation*. Berkley, CA: University of California Press, 1973.

Omark, Donald R., and Joan Good Erickson. *The Bilingual Exceptional Child*. San Diego, CA: College Hill Press, Inc., 1983.

Plata, Maximino. *Assessment, Placement, and Programming of Bilingual Exceptional Pupils: A Practical Approach*. Reston, VA: The Council for Exceptional Children, 1986.

Roseberry-McKibbin, C.A., and G.E. Eicholtz. "Serving Children with Limited English Proficiency in the Schools: A National Survey." *LSHSS* 25(3), pp. 156-164.

Shrybman, James A. *Due Process in Special Education*. Rockville, MD: Aspen Systems Corp., 1982.

Taylor, Orlando L., ed. *Nature of Communication Disorders in Culturally and Linguistically Diverse Populations*. San Diego, CA: College Hill Press, 1986.

Taylor, Orlando L. *Treatment of Communication Disorders in Culturally and Linguistically Diverse Populations*. San Diego, CA: College Hill Press, 1986.

Taylor, Orlando L., and Kay T. Payne. "Culturally Valid Testing: A Proactive Approach." *Topics in Language Disorders*, June 1983.

Taylor, Orlando L., Kay T. Payne, and Noma B. Anderson. "Distinguishing Between Communication Disorders and Communication Differences." *Topics in Language Disorders*, June 1983.

Vaughn-Cooke, Fay Boyd. "Improving Language Assessment in Minority Children." *ASHA*, September 1983.

Williams, Ronald, and Walt Wolfram. *Social Dialects: Differences vs. Disorders*. Rockville, MD: American Speech and Hearing Association, ASHA Committee on Communication Behavior and Problems in Urban Populations (undated document).

Wolfram, Walt. *Speech Pathology and Dialect Differences*. Arlington: VA: Center for Applied Linguistics, 1979.

Cultural Considerations

Second Language Learning
African American: What's in a name?
Hmong Culture
References

Introduction

"All human beings are members of at least one indigenous culture, and they have the capacity to acquire knowledge of other cultures, which may either alter their indigenous cultural norms or permit them to shift from one set of cultural norms to those of some other culture" (Penalosa, 1981, as cited in Taylor, 1986).

It is the task of speech and language pathologists to try to understand students' behavior by viewing their behaviors from their own cultural contexts. Speech and language pathologists also must face issues confronting linguistically and culturally diverse populations and focus on learning and language issues. A child's cultural background and cultural style may influence the way the child interacts and responds in school. As a result, it may be difficult to evaluate or draw conclusions about a student's strengths and weaknesses in the absence of information about the student's cultural background. Figure 2 outlines some cultural parameters "that represent differences between a student's cultural background and that of mainstream culture schools" (Damico and Hamayan, 1992, p. 25). These factors are not considered static, but rather on a continuum.

 Figure 2

Cultural Factors that may affect Educational Performance

(Adapted from *Multicultural Language Intervention: Addressing Cultural and Linguistic Diversity* by J.S. Damico and E.V. Hamayan. Buffalo, NY: Educom Associates, Inc., 1992.)

Educational action	*Other cultures*	*Mainstream culture*
movement	active	passive
space	close	distant
time	untimed	timed
activities	polychronic	monochronic
goal structures	cooperative	competitive
gender role	distinct	similar
role	group	individual
focus of control	external	internal
perceptual style	field dependent	field independent
cognitive style	intuitive	reflective
acculturation	contact	adaptation
language patterns	mismatch	match
language loss	extensive	minimal
code switching	frequent	infrequent
language variance	nonstandard	standard

Culture also shapes a person's reality—a person's view of the world. Cultural, knowledge and experience shape behaviors and influence expectations for and interpretations of other people's behaviors. Thus, a behavior attributed to culture often is based on knowledge of a person's own culture and comparisons with people from differing cultures. Lack of knowledge of, or insensitivity to, cultural differences often results in misperceptions, miscommunication, and cultural stereotyping. Figure 3 lists some aspects of world views that affect assessment and instruction in an educational setting (Erickson, 1993).

Figure 3

The Relationship Between Culture and Communication Styles

(Reprinted with permission from Joan Erickson, "Communicative Disorders in Multicultural Populations." Wisconsin Speech Langugae Hearing Association Convention, May 1993.)

Areas in which culture is manifested	*Areas in which culture influences communication styles*
Family structure	Need and rules for eye contact
Important events in life cycle	Space between speakers
Roles of individual members	Gender, age, and status roles
Rules of interpersonal interactions used	Type and amount of facial expressions
Religious beliefs	Silence as a communication device
Standard for hygiene	Laughter as a communication device
Definitions of health and illness	Address forms
Food preferences	How to open and close a conversation
Dress and personal appearance	Politeness rules
History and traditions	When and how to interrupt
Holidays and celebrations	Turn taking during conversation
Education	Appropriate topics of conversation
Perceptions of work and play	Greetings and leavings
Perceptions of time and space	Humor and when to use it
Explanation of natural phenomena course	Logical ordering of events during dis-
Attitudes toward pets and animals	
Artistic and musical values and tastes	
Life expectancies and aspirations	
Communication and linguistic rules	

Speech and language pathologists must be sensitive to cultural factors that may influence their view of a student's performance, but they also must be cognizant of general philosophical principles that offer a better understanding of linguistic and cultural diversity. The following philosophical principles are adapted from Orlando Taylor's discussion of "Pragmatic Considerations in Addressing Race, Ethnicity, and Cultural Diversity Within the Academy" in *Multicultural Literacy in Communication Disorders: A Manual for Teaching Cultural Diversity within the Professional Education Curriculum.*

• "Race" and "culture" are not the same. Race is a statement about one's biological attributes. Culture is a statement about one's behavior attributes in such diverse areas as values, perceptions, world views, cognitive styles, institutions, language, and so on.

• Within all races there are many cultures. Likewise, culture is not one and the same as nationality, language, or religion, although each is associated with culture. Within every culture there are many internal variations; variations typically associated with such factors as age, gender, socioeconomic status, education, religion, and very importantly, exposure to, and adoption of, other cultural norms.

• Within every culture there may exist differences in the language varieties spoken by that culture. For example, while English is the typical language spoken by contemporary African Americans in the United States, many varieties (dialects) of English are spoken within the group. Thus, for example, the term "Black dialect" ignores the diversity of English use among African Americans, even with respect to vernacular forms.

• There is great overlap among cultures. Both similarities and differences exist across various cultures. An overemphasis on similarity or differences distorts reality with respect to culture and cultural diversity.

- What seems to be logical, sensible, important and reasonable to a person in one culture may seem stupid, irrational, and unimportant to an outsider.
- Feelings of apprehension, loneliness, and lack of confidence are common when encountering another culture.
- Differences between cultures are often seen as threatening and described in negative terms. This tendency must be avoided at all costs.
- Personal observations and reports of other cultures should be regarded with a great deal of skepticism. One should make up one's own mind about another culture and not rely upon reports and experiences of others.
- Stereotyping of a culture is probably inevitable in the absence of frequent contact or study. Experience, as well as study, is required to understand the many subtleties of another culture. Understanding another culture is a continuous and not a discreet process.
- The feelings people have for their own language or dialect are not often evident until they encounter another language or dialect. People often feel that their own language or dialect is far superior to other languages or dialects. Indeed, it is necessary to know the language or dialect of a culture to understand that culture in depth.

Taylor also recommends that speech and language pathologists and other educators consider how they communicate their personal views on culture. He recommends the following considerations.

- Learn the name of any given culture as assigned by its members and use that name.
- Avoid the use of generic terminology as substitutes or synonyms for more descriptive racial/ethnic terms such as "minority" to refer to African Americans, "bilingual" to refer to Hispanic Americans, or "culturally diverse" or "multicultural" to avoid saying non-white.
- Avoid the use of terms that carry multiple meanings and may be offensive to members of non-white groups. The term "minority" is denigrating and suggests numerical importance.
- The use of language that suggests cultural disadvantage of a group suggests disrespect for that culture. Conversely, all European Americans should not be referred to as racist, ethnocentric, middle-class, or speakers of standard English.
- Not all European Americans are incompetent with regard to the topic of cultural diversity, nor are all non-European Americans competent on the topic.
- Be aware of words, images, and situations that suggest that all or most members of a racial or ethnic group are the same. (For example, presumption that all African Americans speak Black English vernacular, or that all Asian Americans are innately competent in math or science.)
- Avoid using unnecessary qualifiers that reinforce racial and ethnic stereotypes. Be aware of offensive ethnic clichés such as "Chinese fire drill" and "Indian-giver".
- Expressions such as "Asian people are so disciplined" or "Black speech is so musical" are patronizing.

In addition to reviewing potential cultural variables prior to working with students and families from diverse cultural backgrounds, speech and language pathologists must become familiar with working definitions of bilingualism and language proficiency. This will assist with the understanding of the relationship between language and culture for African Americans and Hmong. Language can only be studied and assessed as a culturally and socially embedded phenomenon; it must be considered in context. Recognition of this relationship is basic in order to understand and preserve the complexity of language use (Crago and Cole, 1991). Jerome Bruner (1990) writes in *Acts of Meaning* that meaning itself is a culturally mediated phenomenon. Although language and culture are discussed somewhat separately in this guide, they are inextricably intertwined throughout society.

Second Language Learning

In Wisconsin, the number of students with limited-English proficiency (LEP) continues to grow. As these students acquire proficiency in English, they become bilingual or multilingual. Bilingual describes people who are exposed to two languages and who come from homes where a language other than that of the dominant culture has been used. The term bilingual is derived from the Middle English prefix "bi" meaning "two," and the Medieval Latin word "lingua," which means "tongue." In *Language in the Process of Cultural Assimilation and Structural Incorporation of Linguistic Minorities*, Tove Skutnabb-Kangas and P. Toukomas indicate that there are three types of bilingualism.

• proficient bilingualism, or high level of proficiency in two languages
• partial bilingualism, or a native-like level of proficiency in one language (also termed "language dominance") and a low level of proficiency in another
• limited bilingualism, or a low level of proficiency in two languages.

It is also possible that an individual may prefer the use of one language over another without regard to proficiency in the preferred language.

Bilingual language acquisition proceeds either simultaneously or sequentially. In simultaneous acquisition, a child is exposed to two languages from birth. Sequential acquisition occurs when an individual is exposed to one language from birth and a second language at a later time (Cheng, 1991).

Whether a child acquires two or more languages sequentially or simultaneously, the process of acquisition is similar. An important influence on second-language acquisition is the age of the second-language learner. Stephen O. Krashen (1982) further reports that older learners learn more quickly in the early stages of second-language acquisition, however, younger learners tend to attain higher levels of proficiency in the second language.

Additional factors that influence second-language learning and therefore affect the level of proficiency achieved include:

• linguistic factors such as phonological or word order interference of the first language upon the second
• sociolinguistic factors such as familial or peer pressure to learn the second language
• cultural factors such as perception of the second language
• psychosocial influences including the "silent" period, self-confidence, motivation, anxiety, and school or work adjustments
• educational factors including the educational level of parents and their view of education, as well as previous educational history
• immigration and family factors such as date of arrival, reason for immigration, and life in other countries

Social language skills are typically learned first. There are three phases of social language learning in the acquisition of a second language. In phase one, the non-native speaker addresses speakers of the dominant language in his or her native language. This may last from two to three days, or even longer for children. Eventually it is realized that communication cannot occur in two mutually exclusive languages. A silent period, during which the speaker abruptly ceases verbal interactions with the speaker of the dominant language, may ensue. During this phase, attention is focused on listening and comprehension, with interactions usually being non-verbal.

Phase two is marked by the reinitiation of verbal interactions with speakers of the second language. Utterances contain one or two words, usually nouns or names of objects. Other phrases are memorized routines, idioms, or repetitions of other people. This period may last from one to more than 24 weeks.

Phase three is characterized by a shift from repetition to actual production of simple sentences, however, early utterances are typically ungrammatical in form. The later part of this phase is identified by spontaneous dialogue and composition. Vocabulary and syntactic skills develop.

Though these three early phases of second-language acquisition can be identified, it is apparent that "proficiency" in a second language must entail additional skill.

Language proficiency refers to a person's ability to use language effectively in various contexts and to meet the language demands of the situation. D. Hymes states in his discussion of ethnography (1982) that language proficiency refers to knowing how to "say the right thing, in the right way, to the right people in the right place."

James Cummins (1981, 1984) proposes a mode of language proficiency that considers communication embedded in the contexts in which it occurs. In his model, language proficiency is achieved on a situational continuum from context-embedded (face-to-face, social communication) to context-reduced (academic) situational demands.

The context-embedded type of language proficiency is often referred to as Basic Interpersonal Communication Skill (BICS). This is the kind of proficiency required for social communication where much of the information is embedded in the context of the situation. BICS proficiency is the kind of skill demonstrated by children on the playground as they chat in informal situations. Cummins explains that this everyday communication is informal, and students learn and may rely on contextual clues.

On the other end of the continuum is Cognitive Academic Language Proficiency (CALP). This proficiency is usually demanded of children in an academic situation where less information is derived from the context (thus, context-reduced). CALP requires that children derive their understanding exclusively from the language used to convey the message. Situational clues are limited or absent.

In *Assessing Asian Language Performance: Guidelines for Evaluating Limited- English Proficient Students*, Lily Cheng cites Cummins, who maintains that BICS level of proficiency is acquired in two years on the average. However, it may take as many as five to seven years (or more) to achieve proficiency for cognitive and academic language demands. As a result, children learning English as a second language may appear to be English proficient in casual conversations but fail in the classroom or in other context-reduced situations.

Children need to acquire proficiencies all along the BICS-CALP continuum to succeed academically. Cummins maintains that children who exit English as a Second Language (ESL) programs have likely achieved BICS-type proficiencies, but their CALP proficiencies may be inadequate for functioning in academic situations.

Michael Canale (1984) offers another view of English as a second language proficiency that suggests that language proficiency is a multi-dimensional construct. In the book *Language Proficiency and Academic Achievement*, Canale contrasts this with a unidimensional framework which considers only the structural components of language (for example, phonology, orthography, morphology, syntax, and semantics) and ignores the different language demands required in various contexts (for example, pragmatic and discourse skills).

Canale suggests that there are three dimensions of language proficiency.
• basic language proficiency involving the biological universals required for language development and use
• communicative language proficiency involving the social and interpersonal uses of language through spoken or written channels
• autonomous language proficiency involving problem-solving, organization of ideas, monitoring one's own thoughts, and so forth.

Each dimension is characterized by several communicative competencies, including grammatical, socio-linguistic strategies (for example, conversational repair strategies), and discourse (construction of meaning across sentence boundaries) competencies.

Both Cummins and Canale stress the need to look beyond social communication skills when evaluating language in the school environment. It is necessary to view proficiency as the ability to use language effectively across a range of communicative contexts. Programs emphasizing only social communication and language structure may exit ESL students too soon. Lack of higher-level language and discourse skills may contribute to the failure of ESL students in English-only instructional settings.

14

African American: What's in a name?

When describing the ethnicity of persons of color in the United States, it is often difficult to determine which terms are more appropriate to use. For African Americans, several terms have been used interchangeably over the last 100 years. In the late 1800s, *negro* and *colored* were the acceptable terms to use when describing persons of African decent. During the early 1900s, Marcus Garveyt, the founder and leader of the Universal Negro Improvement Association (founded in 1911), began to encourage his members to use the word "black" to describe themselves because it expressed unity between persons of African descent throughout the world. In the 1950s, Malcom X (of the Nation of Islam) and other prominent black leaders began using the word as a symbol of pride, and as a means to unify African Americans politically in the United States during the early days of the Civil Rights Movement.

With the advancement of the "Black Power" movement during the 1960s and 70s, "Black" quickly replaced "Negro" as the more acceptable term to use when describing black people. Nevertheless, during the early 1980s, many blacks began to use African American to express their historical ties to both African and American culture.

Since the 1970s it has become more common to refer to persons of color who are primarily of African ancestry as African American, the term "black" continues to be used interchangeably with "African American" in both writing an conversation. This is similar to the way in which Native American and American Indian are used to describe populations indigenous to the United States.

Educators must recognize that "black and proud" is an historical statement of the past. Once the preferred term was colored, then it was Negro and Afro-American. Black reflected the growing self-determination of the 1960s. "Now, African American must reflect the cultural integrity and a higher level of consciousness of the future. Black is to African American in the 1990s what Negro was to black in the mid-1960s. New terms are no more than an attempt by people to connect themselves to a present agenda. The lack of common professional terminology in the classroom can tear teachers between attempts to be sensitive and recognize individual cultures and attempts not to stereotype or impart negative images in children" (Gill, 1991, p. 28).

This is extremely important because, as Orlando Taylor suggests in *Treatment of Communication Disorders in Culturally and Linguistically Diverse Populations* "there is perhaps no cultural group with greater diversity" than African Americans. African Americans "cut across all socioeconomic classes; religions; skin colors; political persuasions; and social beliefs and traditions." Figure 4 specifies behaviors that may be interpreted differently by members of various cultures.

■ **Figure 4**

Behavioral Factors that may affect Interpretation by Individuals

(Adapted from *Treatment of Communication Disorders in Culturally and Linguistically Diverse Populations* by Orlando Taylor. San Diego, CA: College Hill Press, 1986.) Warning: Remember that generalizations can be dangerous as they often do not apply when considering individual students.

African American	*Opposing View*
• Touching of one's hair by another person is often considered offensive.	• Touching of one's hair by another person is a sign of affection.
• Preference for indirect eye contact during speaking is a sign of attentiveness and respect.	• Preference for direct eye contact during listening and indirect eye contact during speaking are sign of attention and respect.
• Public behavior may be emotionally intense, dynamic, and demonstrative.	• Public behavior is expected to be modest and emotionally restrained. Emotional displays are seen as irresponsible or in bad taste.
• A clear distinction exists between argument and fight. Verbal "sparring" is not necessarily a precursor to violence.	• Heated arguments suggest that violence is imminent.
• Asking personal questions of someone a person has met for the first time is seen as improper and intrusive.	• Inquiring about jobs, family, and so forth of someone a person has met for the first time is seen as friendly.
• The use of direct questions is sometimes seen as harassment (for example, asking when something will be finished is seen as rushing that person to finish).	• Use of direct questions for personal information is permissible.
• Interruption during conversation is usually tolerated. Access to speaking is granted to the person who is most assertive.	• Rules of turn-taking in conversation dictate that one person speaks at a time until all of that person's points are made.
• Conversations are regarded as private between the recognized participants. Butting in is seen as eavesdropping and is not tolerated.	• Adding points of information or insights to a conversation in which a person is not engaged is seen as being helpful.
• Accusations or allegations are general rather than categorical and are not intended to be all-inclusive. Refutation is the responsibility of the accused.	• Stereotypical accusations or allegations are all-inclusive. Refutation or making exception is the responsibility of the person making the accusation.
• Silence denotes refutation of accusation. To state that you feel accused is regarded as an admission of guilt.	• Silence denotes acceptance of an accusation. Guilt is verbally denied.

African-American Culture

To fully comprehend the essence of the African American presence in the history and culture of the United States, it is necessary to examine the enculturative and aculturative dimensions of African American life. It is necessary to focus on the entrenchment of African customs and the amalgamation of different African cultures as different immigrants from different countries and tribal groups and how they interacted during their slavery on plantations. Furthermore, the gradual merger of African ways with Anglo Saxon customs and European habits has added to the scope of African American life.

The earliest African Americans arrived in the 1620s as indentured servants. Most African Americans came to the United States as slaves, beginning in 1630 (Scott, 1995).

Because the first African immigrants to America had experienced a rich history of social, cultural, economic, and political development that began long before many Western Europe civilizations, they knew first hand the rise and fall of great kingdoms. Not only were they from different tribes and countries, they spoke different languages and dialects.

Despite the diversity among the original African immigrants, these people shared certain commonalities and experiences, including the local community organization, a farming economy, and an extended family structure. They prized cooperation, mutual aid, and the wisdom, experience, and authority of elders. Cultural values and traditions were transmitted through music, folklore, and dance. Tribal history and tradition were transmitted orally. Religion, arts, and crafts were very important and reflected in everyday life activities for the perpetuation of unity and continuity.

Africans reacted to America in different ways depending on their particular African background, geographic location, the ratio of blacks to whites, and so forth. African Americans did not assimilate into the structure of mainstream society but meshed African and European habits, customs, and values to form a distinct cultural system. Alternative institutions and lifestyles resulted from discrimination and the practice of barring Africans from mainstream society.

The family has been the pillar of African American society, socializing its children into the essential African American cultural values and teaching children the skills to survive in a predominately white society. Words continue to be prized devices for survival outside the African American community. An artistic performer is widely respected in the community. It is therefore not surprising that some of the most valued expressions of the culture are music, dance, art, drama, and literature--particularly poetry. However, it is important to point out that African Americans have made great contributions to virtually every phase of American life, including science, medicine, civil engineering (for example, the design of the city of Washington, D.C.), and architecture.

Major contributors include Nanny Helen Burroughs, Dr. W.E.B. Dubois, Booker T. Washington, Mary McLeod Bethune, Carter G. Woodson, Marva Collins, and Molefi Kete Asante in education; Katharine Dunham, Alvin Ailey, and Arthur Mitchell in dance; Rita Deve, Toni Morrison, Zora Neele Hurston, and Walter Moseley in literature; Benjamin Banneker, George Carruthers, Ernest Just and George Washington Carver and Dr. Mae Jemison in science; Scott Joplin, Louis Armstrong, and Bessie Smith in music; Benjamin C. Davis, Colin Powell, Hazel Johnson, Tuskegee Airmen and buffalo soldiers in the military; Charles Alston, Jean-Michel Basquiat, Romare Bearden, John Biggers, Camille Billops, Tom Feelings and Edmonia Lewis in the visual and applied arts; Josephine Baker, Harry Belofante, Bill Cosby, Dorothy Dandaride, Ossie Davis, Ruby Dee, Spike Lee, Melvin Van Peebles, Sidney Portier, and August Wilson in the performing arts; and Benjamin Carson, Charles Drew, Joycelyn Elders, and Percy Lavon Julian in medicine (Scott, 1995).

Researchers have described learning style differences that have their roots in culture. Knowledge of these factors helps educators understand an African American child's culture, language, and learning patterns. Such knowledge helps speech and language pathologists determine differences from disorders. Janice Hale-Benson (1982) summarizes the work of Rosalie Cohen and Asa Hilliard in describing two cognitive styles: analytical and relational. Figure 5 offers some characteristics of each style.

Many African American people use the relational cognitive style. However, the use of either style is not confined exclusively to any ethnic group or social class. Every group includes different style users. In *Black Children: Their Roots, Cultural, and Learning Style*, Janice Hale-Benson suggests that children develop their cognitive styles through the socialization they receive in their families and through the experiences and friendships their families support. Thus, the roots of cognitive style are embedded in an individual's cultural background. A child's "native ability" does not determine his or her cognitive style. Traditionally, schools have valued and fostered skills clustered in the analytical style of information processing.

Figure 5

Learning Styles Rooted in Culture

Warning: Remember that generalizations can be dangerous as they often do not apply when considering individual students.

Analytical Style

- Stimulus-centered
- Parts-specific
- Finds non-obvious attributes
- Abstracts common or generalizable principle of a stimulus
- Notices formal properties of stimulus that have relatively stable and long-lasting meanings
- Ignores the idiosyncratic
- Extracts from embedded context
- Names extracted properties and gives them meaning in themselves
- Relationships tend to be linear
- Relationships that are noticed tend to be static and descriptive rather than functional or inferentia.
- Relationships seldom involved process or motivation as a basis for relations
- Perception on conceptual distance between observers and observed.
- An objective attitude—a belief that everything takes place "out there" in the stimulus
- Stimulus viewed as formal, long-lasting, and relatively constant; therefore, opportunity exists to study it in detail
- Long attention span
- Greater perceptual vigilance
- A reflective attitude and relatively sedentary nature
- Language style is standard English of controlled elaboration
- Language depends upon relatively long-lasting and stable meanings of words
- Language depends upon formal and stable rules of organization
- Communications are intended to be understood in themselves (for example, without dependence upon non-verbal cues or idiosyncratic context)
- "Part of speech" can readily be seen in nonsense sentences
- Analytic speech characterized by "hesitation phenomena"; pauses for verbal planning by controlled vocal modulation and revision of sentence organization to convey specific meaning, since words have formal meanings

Relational Style

- Self-centered
- Global
- Fine descriptive characteristics
- Identifies the unique
- Ignores commonalities
- Embedded for meaning
- Relevant concepts must have special or personal relevance to observer
- Meanings are unique, depending upon immediate context
- Generalizations and linear notions are generally unused and devalued
- Parts of the stimulus and its non-obvious attributes are not given names and appear to have no meanings in themselves
- Relationships tend to be functional and inferential
- Since emphasis is placed on the unique and the specific, the global, and the discrete, on notions of difference rather than on variation or common things, the search for mechanism to form abstract generalizations is not stimulated
- Responses tend to be affective
- Perceived conceptual distance between the observer and the observed is narrow
- The field is perceived as responding to the person
- The field may have a life of its own
- Personification of the inanimate
- Distractible
- Emotional
- Over-involved in all activities
- Easily angered by minor frustrations
- Immediacy of response
- Short attention span
- Gestalt learners
- Descriptive abstraction for word selection
- Words must be embedded in specific time-bound context for meaning
- Few synonyms in language
- Language dependent upon unique context and upon many interactional characteristics of the communicants on time and place, on inflection, muscular movements, and other non-verbal cues
- Fluent spoken language

Figure 5 (cont.)

Learning Styles Rooted in Culture

Analytical Style	*Relational Style*
• Sometimes view of self expressed as an aspect of roles, such as function to be performed • View of self tends to be in terms of status role	• Strong, colorful expressions • Wide range of meaningful vocal intonation and inflection • Condensed conditions, sensitivity to hardly perceptible variations of mood and tone in other individuals and in their surroundings • Poor response to timed, scheduled, preplanned activities that interfere with immediacy of response • Tends to ignore structure • Self-descriptions tend to point to essence

Hale-Benson argues that certain features of the relational and analytic modes make it difficult for a child to develop characteristics that are present in the other mode. Learned behavior, language, interpersonal patterns, values, beliefs, and the general cultural context of a person determines his or her cognitive style. Learning about aspects of other cognitive styles may help an individual change or modify his or her cognitive style.

The analytic style suggests that the universe is organized in a linear fashion—time is on a continuum, social space is a linear hierarchy; events result from multiple causality. This assumption of linearity is not found among children who use a relational learning style. For these children, time is a series of discrete moments, not a continuum. They consider themselves in the center of space rather than in a position relative to others. They perceive specific causality of events rather than multiple causality. Similarly, many aspects of African and African American culture have been described as organized in a circular fashion, in contrast to the linear organization of Western culture. Music, language, and other performing arts are used as examples of circular versus linear organization.

Hale-Benson (1982) provides the following list describing the African American cultural style.
• African American people tend to respond to things in terms of the whole picture instead of its parts. The Euro-American tends to believe that anything can be divided and subdivided into pieces and that these pieces add up to a whole.
• African American people tend to prefer inferential reasoning to deductive or inductive reasoning.
• African American people tend to approximate space, numbers, and time rather than stick to accuracy.
• African American people tend to prefer to focus on people and their activities rather than on things. This tendency is shown by the fact that so many
  —African American people have a keen sense of justice and are quick to analyze and perceive injustice.
  —African American people tend to lean toward altruism, a concern for one's fellow man.
  —African American people tend to prefer novelty, freedom, and personal distinctiveness.
  —African American people in general tend not to be "word" dependent. They tend to be very proficient in non-verbal communications.

The examination of African American cultural style by speech and language pathologists is an important step in understanding the complex nature of this group of Americans. The following discussion of African American English provides additional information on the decision-making process of determining the differentiation between language difference and language disorder.

African-American Culture

One of the major language varieties spoken in the United States is the one most closely associated with African Americans. Most recent labeling of this form includes: Black English, Vernacular Black English, Ebonics, and African American English. Some of the earlier labels included terms such as "substandard," which clearly reflected attitudes about language differences laden with misperceptions and value judgments. This type of thinking leads to erroneous decision making when attempting to distinguish between a language difference and a language disorder.

Speech and language pathologists who deliver services to African American students must be aware that not all African Americans speak African American English and everyone who uses it is not African American (Owens, 1991).

Differences within a language are commonly referred to as dialectical differences. If a person chooses to use this term to describe language differences or variations, it is imperative to have a working definition of the term dialect. In *Dialects and American English*, Walt Wolfram defines dialect as "a neutral label to refer to any variety of language which is shared by a group of speakers. Languages are invariably manifested through their dialects, and to speak a language is to speak some dialect of that language. In this technical usage there are no particular social or attitudinal evaluations of the term (no good or bad); it is simply how we refer to any language variety that typifies a group of speakers within a language."

Some scholars continue to debate the terminology used to describe and categorize African American English. Some prefer the term Ebonics (black sound), which shifts away from a theory of African American English solely as a dialect of Standard English and places more emphasis on African American English as a complete language system with its own rules and structures, having origins that can be traced to the many languages of West Africa.

In the case of West Africans brought to the United States, the slave masters deliberately practiced language mixing by splitting up groups of Africans speaking the same language to prevent the slaves from communicating easily with each other. The slave masters did this as an attempt to minimize cohesiveness and unity among the various groups of Africans and as a disruption to the transmission of their culture.

The most widely accepted theory on the origin and development of African American English is the Creole Hypothesis. In *Dialects and American English*, Wolfram says the major issue concerning the historical development of Vernacular Black English centers around the Creole-origin hypothesis. According to this hypothesis, today's Vernacular Black English developed from a Creole language (a special language developed in language contact situations in which the vocabulary from one primary language is imposed on a specially adapted restricted grammatical structure) used through a good portion of the New World, including the Plantation South.

This Creole was fairly widespread during slavery and persisted to some extent in the antebellum South as well. Those who take this position noted that this Creole was not a unique development that arose in the mainland south, but that it shows continuity with well-known Creoles of the African diaspora such as Krio, spoken today along the coast of West Africa (in Sierra Leone), and the English-based Creolese of the Caribbean, such as Jamaican Creole. The Creole, its vestiges in the United States found in Gullah (more popularly called "geechee"), is still spoken by a small number of blacks in the Sea Islands off the coast of South Carolina and Georgia. It is maintained that this Creole was fairly widespread among blacks on southern plantations, but it was not spoken to any extent by whites.

Over time, through contact with surrounding dialects, this Creole language was modified to become more like other varieties of English, including southern standard varieties, in a process referred to as decreolization. Because this decreolization process was gradual, and not necessarily complete in all its phases, the Creole predecessor is cited as the basis for some present-day characteristics of Vernacular Black English. For example, copula absence (e.g., You ugly) is a well-known trait found in Creole languages, so some people might maintain that the present version of copula absence is a vestigial manifestation of the Creole origin of Vernacular Black English.

Similar arguments have been made for the various types of inflectional-absence in this variety, as well as phonological characteristics such as consonant cluster reduction. Both linguistic traits and social history have been used to argue for the Creole origin of Vernacular Black English. J.L. Dillard's book *Black English: Its History and Usage in the United States* is still the most complete argument for the Creole Hypothesis, although there are more careful accounts of particular linguistic and historical details now offered in support of this hypothesis.

The Niger-Congo-Ebonics Hypothesis places more emphasis on the African elements existing in African American speech. This theory also illustrates that African American speech has undergone processes to become a morphosyntactically, continuous, autonomous language of Africa just as modern English evolved from the language of the German or Anglo-Saxon. Based upon comparative analyses of West African languages, African American speech, and European American speech, the diachronic and synchronic linguistic evidences show that the continuation of an original African linguistic substratum in African American speech is the basis for the differences in African American and European American social dialects.

Although a variety of theories and hypotheses concerning the origins and development of African American English exists, these theories point out that African American English evolved overtime from varied language contact and convergence. By definition, the word convergence implies a coming together. In this convergence of languages, it is often forgotten that African languages have influenced American English and were not abandoned and did not disappear. One example of the African influence on American English is the expression OK, which is a derivation of a West African word pronounced "wa kay."

The awareness of the similarities and differences of these theories help speech and language pathologists understand African American English and its implications for diagnosis and therapy.

It cannot be denied that African American English is a viable, rule-based, and highly structured linguistic system characterized by variations in phonology, morphology/syntax, and semantics. Differences also exist in suprasegmentals and pragmatics or communication style. Linguistic and cultural diversity also impacts on areas such as phonology, voice, and fluency.

The African American English described in Appendix A is to be used as a reference and should be used with other measures (such as gathering information from a family member, primary caregiver, or other members of the person's speech community) that are vitally important to assessment. These forms are often primarily used by working class African Americans in the northern United States and rural African Americans in the southern United States. Not every African American uses African American English and not everyone who uses it is an African American (Owens, 1991). Wolfram states in *Dialects and American English* "although there seems to be a core of non-standard structures, we have to be careful about saying that all speakers in a given vernacular variety exhibit this common set of structures. Not all speakers necessarily use the entire set of structure described and there may be differing patterns of usage among speakers." Thus, the charts in Appendix A are to serve as guidelines while assessing individuals who may be using African American English. (Chapter 3 includes a more extensive discussion of descriptive assessment.)

Hmong Culture

The word Hmong translates as "free man" in English. Traditionally, individuals of Hmong descent were migratory, pioneering people who suffered political oppression for many decades. Originally from China, they migrated south, mostly settling in the highlands. Beginning in the nineteenth century, many left China for the mountainous northern half of what was for some time known as Indochina, as well as Thailand and Burma. In the early 1800s, some arrived in Laos. The people lived primarily in an agrarian society that farmed in the highlands of the countries in which they settled.

The Japanese occupation of Southeast Asia during World War II weakened the French colonial rules in Indochina. That weakness opened the door for many nationalist groups to form their movements to fight for independence (for example, the Ho Chiminh Movement in Vietnam and the Lao Isarath in Laos). However, the French regained strength after the destruction of Hiroshima and Nagasaki, which seriously paralyzed the Japanese domination in that part of the world.

Being reinforced, the French colonial governments in Indochina also began to face resistance from the independent movements. Between 1946 and 1954, many Hmong joined the French to fight against the communist-supported freedom fighters, while others took part to fight for independence. The French opened negotiation with its three colonial countries after they had been defeated at Dien-Bien-Fu in November 1954. Yet the victory and negotiations did not solve the Indochinese problems. Vietnam was divided into North and South with the 17th parallel serving as their border. Hanoi became the capital city of North Vietnam, and Saigon became the capital city of South Vietnam.

A decade later, the United States stepped in to protect South Vietnam from communist domination. Strategically, to protect South Vietnam, the United States had to occupy Laos, but it did not want to send additional troops into that country. In the early 1960s, the Hmong were recruited to operate a series of secret operations as the United States' Special Guerrilla Units. The Hmong held three major responsibilities. They were responsible for rescuing U.S. pilots who were downed along the Lao/Vietnam border by North Vietnamese anti-aircraft; for protecting a U.S. radar system on the Pathee plateau in Central Sam Neua, a northeastern Laotian province; and for blockading the North Vietnamese military convoys along the Hochiminh Trail.

In 1975, the United States pulled out from Southeast Asia, leaving the Hmong--its best ally during that Vietnam conflict—without protection. The Hmong were quickly targeted for systematic elimination due to their connection with the United States. Approximately 100,000 of them fled their homeland to refugee camps in Thailand to escape the extermination campaign, and the United States eventually accepted them as refugees.

There are approximately 150,000 Hmong now living in the United States. In 1996, it was estimated that there were more than 40,000 Hmong living in Wisconsin (Xiong, 1996). Since 1988, the yearly influx of Hmong into Wisconsin has stabilized at about 350 families, or 2,000 individuals, largely coming from the refugee camps in Thailand to be reunited with families in the United States.

In 1996, the camps in Thailand were closed so current movement consists of refugees moving from one community to another. Wisconsin ranks second after California in numbers of Hmong residents. The Wisconsin communities of Milwaukee, Green Bay, Eau Claire, Wausau, Appleton, and Sheboygan hold the greatest concentration of Hmong.

Many Hmong families have achieved social acculturation and economic independence in the United States. Acculturation can be defined as the process of becoming adapted to a new or different culture or the mutual influence of different cultures in close contact. In *Multicultural Language Intervention: Addressing Cultural and Linguistic Diversity*, Jack Damico and Else Hamayan list three phases of acculturation: contact, conflict, and adaptation. These three phases depend upon
• the amount of the time the individual has spent in the target culture (How many years in the United States? in Wisconsin? in schools?)
• the extent to which the exposure has occurred (What is the status of the individual's English?)
• the purposes of the exposure (Has the individual been employed outside of the home? attended school?)
• the receptivity of the host culture (How much does the host culture know about the individual's culture? What are the attitudes and beliefs of each culture?)
• the support provided from the home culture (To what degree is the whole family acculturated? Do they want to change? Do they mind if their child changes? Does the family speak English?)

Damico and Hamayan suggest that school personnel use these principles to estimate the differences between the student's background and the expectations of the school as a way of understanding the relationship between culture and school performance.

Clans and Names

Dr. Dao Yang states in *Hmong at the Turning Point*, "The Hmong mentality has, through the ages, been profoundly steeped in the concept of group. What counts is most often the group—the family, the clan—rather than the individual, whose sojourn on earth is a brief one." The basic unit of the clan is the household. A Hmong household, with the man at the head, might consist of a man's wife or wives, his children, his son's wife or wives and children, and, possibly, children of the next generation. Mentally or physically disabled relatives may be members of a brother's or son's household or clan. All clan members are treated as brothers and sisters. Members of one clan must only marry an individual from another clan. All clan members defer to the clan leader for guidance.

In *Hmong at the Turning Point*, Dao Yang reports 18 patrilineal clan names in Laos: Chang, Cheng, Chu, Fang, Her, Khang, Kong, Kue, Lor or Lo, Ly or Lee, Moua, Pha, Tang, Thao, Vue, Xiong, Vang, and Yang. Clan members adopt their clan names for official purposes. "Considerable variation exists in English spellings of Hmong names. American and French interviewers wrote the names phonetically as best they could. Some standardization, however incorrect, has taken place in the American spellings over the past few years" (Yang, 1993).

Some children receive a given name at a special naming ceremony three days after their birth. Children are not given a middle name as in the Western sense. If a child's name is Ying Xiong, Ying is her given name and Xiong is the clan to which she belongs. If the child's name is Kou Neng Moua, Kou Neng is her given name and Moua is the clan to which she belongs. Neng is not a middle name, and should be used whenever addressing the child (for example, Kou Neng).

The Hmong word for girl is chai and the Hmong word for boy is tou. Often a child is addressed by those designations in the family as well as by the given name. For Tou See Vue or Chai Kou Neng Moua, See and Kou Neng are part of the given names not middle names. When a child socializes, either the given name or surname (clan name) may be used in the first position, depending on the individual's preference. Hmong individuals living in Laos use the clan name in the first position, as that is the tradition in Laos (Lo, 1994).

When a man is "established," reaching a time in life that involves responsibility, such as being a parent, an "honorable" name is given. An example of a man's name is

Given Name: Sao
Clan Name: Thao
Honorable Name: Chu
Possible Mature Name: Chu Sao Thao (Morrow, 1989)

When a woman becomes a mother, she may be called Nia (mother), adding either her first child's name or her husband's name. An example is:

Full Name: May Xee Vang
First Child's Name: Soua
Husband's Name: Sue
Two Possible Names: Soua Nia (Soua's mother) or Nia Sue (Sue's wife)

A woman also considers herself a part of her father's clan. She often will use her father's clan name, which can cause confusion (Morrow, 1989). According to Choua Lo, an interpreter and translator, this confusion mentioned by Morrow only happens for those unfamiliar with the complexities of the Hmong culture.

Information about names is very important. Proper use of a Hmong child's and parents' names can contribute to developing good rapport and serve as the beginning of a positive relationship between the school and family. Figure 6 (adapted from R.D. Morrow's "What's in a Name: In Particular a Southeast Asian Name?" in the September 1989 issue of *Young Children*) provides suggestions for addressing Hmong children and their parents.

How to Address Hmong Children and Their Parents

Always

• Recognize the differences in names among Hmong people and other Southeast Asian groups.
• Learn to pronounce names clearly, correctly, and in the Southeast Asian way.
• Teach children to write their names in the American way.
• Respect the special quality of given names.
• Recognize that a family name may be placed first as an emphasis of a person's roots.
• Determine if the family has chosen to "Americanize" the use of the family name. If so, call the children by their preferred names.
• Respect the child's choice of name.

Never

• Assume all Southeast Asian names are used the same way.
• Call a child "Yang," "Xiong," or "Vue," as it is improper to address a child by the family name.
• Neglect to show children the differences in writing names in the American and Hmong ways.
• Treat names as unimportant.
• Minimize the importance placed on the families' roots.
• Assume that all Hmong people will prefer the use of their given name only.
• Change the name in an effort to Anglicize it. For example, do not call "Mai" "May."

Individual Differences

As with all cultural, ethnic, and societal groups, it is important to remember that all individuals in the Hmong community do not have the same goals, objectives, behaviors, experiences, beliefs, and levels of literacy.

Despite their rich oral histories, as well as legends and folk tales that have been passed down from one generation to another, it is believed the Hmong language did not appear in written form until the 1950s. Formal education was not available to many of the people and, because those who were able to attend school were taught in Lao or French, many still cannot read or write their own language. As a result, many have few prior educational or vocational skills and experiences to draw upon beyond home embroidery (and other types of needlework), farming, and warfare. The elderly, the unskilled, the illiterate, and those with large families may experience more difficulty adapting to the "modern" world and are largely unprepared for salaried employment (Cheng, 1991). However, those individuals who had access to formal education prior to coming to the United States are often multilingual and literate in several languages including Hmong (Hmoob/Leng and Hmoob Dawb), Lao, French, Thai, and English.

Hmong students who have come from refugee camps and those who were born in the United States may have observable differences. For example, some students who came from the refugee camps may be passive learners. They were not encouraged to develop questioning skills; they learned by watching and imitating other children and adults. They were not to question teachers. Some children experienced psychological turmoil and also witnessed atrocities while living in the camps. Some may become confused between the mixed messages of being quiet and cooperative (the Hmong cultural message) while being expected to actively participate in learning in American schools (the American academic message).

Many of the children born in the United States participate in school much like their Caucasian peers (Xiong, 1994). While some students strive for academic excellence to bring honor to their households, others feel isolated, rejected, or confused as an ethnic minority in American schools. They may experience frustration due to language problems and misunderstandings, and they may be extremely quiet, indicating possible depression and withdrawal, not disobedience. Such behavior also may be because their parents are not connected to the dominant culture as they struggle to balance old ways with new ways. Traditional verbal coping approaches may not be successful for these students.

As Figure 7 shows, other behaviors may simply be sociocultural differences appropriate to the particular culture.

 Figure 7

Sociocultural Differences

(Reprinted with permission from "Referring Culturally Different Children: Sociocultural Considerations" in *Academic Therapy* 20:4, pages 503-509. Further information about sociocultural considerations may be found in *Human Ecology and Cognitive Style: Comparative Studies in Cultural and Psychological Adaptation* by J.W. Berry; *Culturally Diverse Exceptional Children*, edited by J.N. Nazzaro; and *Acculturation: Theory, Models, and Some New Findings*, edited by A. Padilla.)

General Area	*Selected Indicating Behaviors*	*Sociocultural Considerations*
Withdrawn Behaviors	Not responding when spoken to Fails to talk, though has skill Prefers to be alone	Normal stage in second language and adaptation to new culture Culturally appropriate to native culture
Defensive Behaviors	Loses belongings Exhibits "I don't care" attitude Lacks responsibility Wastes time Arrives late Cheats Blames others Difficulty in changing attitudes	Presupposes familiarity with having belongings Adapting to new culture may cause anxiety and resistance to change Concepts of time vary considerably from culture to culture External locus of control may be taught or encouraged in some cultures Exteral vs. internal locus of control; confusion results from adapting to new culture
Disorganized Behaviors	Confused in terms of time Poor living skills Poor interpersonal relationships and adaptation to new culture	Concepts of time vary considerably from culture to culture Culturally appropriate to native culture Normal stage in second language acquisition
Aggressive Behaviors	Talks out in class Fights or harasses others Impulsive behavior Talks back to teacher Does not follow class rules	Culturally appropriate in native culture Presupposes familiarity with apropriate school behavior and language

---

Serious educational problems occur when young Hmong women leave school to marry and become mothers. It may not be unusual for a 15-year-old girl to have a child, because early marriage and motherhood are still common and accepted in the culture. Young men, on the other hand, often receive more encouragement than the women to pursue formal education. These practices, with regard to the young women, are happening with less frequency as families become more acculturated.

Many Hmong children are doing well in Wisconsin schools. When a child is experiencing school problems, it may be related to possible cultural conflicts or how the culture influences the rules of language use. Figure 8 lists some cultural influences specific to some Asian social and cultural contexts. These do not apply to the school setting or outside of social contexts within a particular culture (Xiong, 1994) but are provided for cultural awareness.

■ **Figure 8**

Cultural Influences Specific to some Asian Social and Cultural Contexts

(Adapted from *Treatment of Communication Disorders in Culturally and Linguistically Diverse Populations* by Orlando Taylor. San Diego, CA: College Hill Press, 1986.)

Asian	*Anglo-American*
Touching or hand-holding between bers of the same sex is acceptable	Touching or hand-holding between members mem- of the same sex may be considered as a sign of homosexuality
Hand-holding, hugging, kissing between men and women in public is acceptable	Hand-holding, hugging, kissing between men and women in public looks ridiculous
A slap on the back is insulting	A slap on the back denotes friendliness
It is not customary to shake hands with persons of the opposite sex	It is customary to shake hands with persons of the opposite sex
Waving motions are used only by adults to call little children and not vice-versa	Waving motions are often used to call both children and adults

---

Parent-School Relationships

Positive relationships between families and schools are important for all students. In the refugee camps in Thailand, Hmong parents did not interact with teachers. Instead, their primary role was to provide food, shelter, clothing, and other physical necessities for their children. However, in America, most Hmong parents do participate in the education of their children, in addition to continuing to attend to their physical needs.

Some parents frequently appear resistant to or confused about special educational programs. In their culture, pride and shame are strong principles that have a tremendous impact on the household. Students who are doing well reflect positively-valued behavior on the family. A student who has been identified as having problems exhibits negatively-valued behavior on the family, resulting in collective family shame. Figures 9 and 10 provide background information relative to generalities associated with some culturally based Asian attitudes toward education and parental expectations of their children and the educational system.

When school personnel speak with Hmong parents about school issues, they must explain the American views on which school performance concepts are based. They also must explain the educational terms they use, preferably through a competent bilingual interpreter. The Hmong language does not contain words that differentiate between a child's potential to perform and the child's actual performance. The culture has developed no words for concepts such as learning disability, articulation, or language delay. Some Hmong words reflect school performance. For example, kawm ntawv tuav means it takes a child longer to learn new information. Cim xeeb tsi zoo means poor memory—a child may learn something but later forget it (Xiong, 1994).

■ **Figure 9**

Asian Attitudes Toward Education

(Reprinted with permission from *Assessing Asian Language Performance: Guidelines for Evaluating Limited-English Proficient Students* by L.L. Cheng. Oceanside, CA: Academic Communication Associates, 1991.)

Asian Cultural Themes	Educational Implications
Education is a formal process	Students are to engage in serious academic work
Teachers are to behave formally and are expected to lecture and provide information	Teachers are not to be interrupted
Teachers are to be highly respected	Students are reluctant to ask questions
Humility is an important virtue	Students are not to "show off" or volunteer information
Reading of factual information is valuable study	Reading of fiction is not considered serious study
It is important for students to be orderly and obedient	Students are to sit quietly and listen attentively
Students learn by observations and memorization	Rote memory is an effective teaching tool
Pattern practice and rote learning are "studying"	Homework in pattern practice is important and is expected
Children must respect adults	Children are expected to listen to adults
Children must respect authority	Teachers are not to be challenged or questioned
Teachers have authority and control	The class is run in an orderly manner and is highly controlled
Rote learning is preferred over discovery learning	Students do well in sheltered and structured activity—less peer interaction and group projects, more lectures and instruction
Teachers are carriers of knowledge and are transmitters of information	Students are expected to work in a quiet environment and are not be roam freely around the classroom
Schooling is a serious process	Students avoid confrontation
Harmony is an important virtue	

■ **Figure 10**

Inconsistencies between U.S. Teachers' Expectations and Asian Parents' Expectations

(Reprinted with permission from *Assessing Asian Language Performance: Guidelines for Evaluating Limited-English Proficient Students* by L.L. Cheng. Oceanside, CA: Academic Communication Associates, 1991.)

U.S. Teachers' Expectations	Asian Parents' Expectations
Students need to participate in classroom activities and discussion	Students are to be quiet and obedient
Students need to be creative	Students should be told what to do
Students learn through inquiries and debate	Students learn through memorization and observation
Asian students generally do well on their own	Teachers need to teach, students need to study
Critical thinking is important. Analytical thinking is important.	It is important to deal with the real world
Creativity and fantasy are to be encouraged	Factual information is important; fantasy is not
Problem solving is important	Students should be taught the steps to solve problems
Students need to ask questions	Teachers are not to be challenged
	Reading is the decoding of information and facts

Hmong parents may view a child's disability as a punishment for sins and transgressions committed by them or other relatives. Hmong people also believe dietary choices during pregnancy, failure to properly worship ancestors, or curses by evil spirits may cause physical deformities, developmental disabilities, or cleft palate. Some people may believe that it is their turn to have a deaf child born to them (Bliatou, et al., 1988). Older Hmong families have not had much experience with severe disabilities, since these children often did not survive in Laos.

School personnel must recognize the family's need for saving face because of cultural beliefs regarding disabilities. Because many parents rarely question educators' decisions, parents must have ample opportunity to talk "around" the issue of disability (McInnis, et al, 1990). School personnel will need to show families that a child has the capacity to change or improve his or her school performance.

School personnel should have an understanding and appreciation of Hmong spiritual beliefs when a student exhibits problems that indicate a need for medical referral. Hmong culture has very specific beliefs related to illness and health care. The people believe there are five main explanations of illness, including illnesses with a natural or organic basis, those illnesses caused by supernatural or metaphysical factors, and illnesses of a magical origin. Some Hmong parents may consult a Shaman or an herbalist, combined with the American health care system (Western medicine). The longer the Hmong people are in the United States, the more likely they are to use the American health care system. More information is available in *The Hmong in America: Providing Ethnic-Sensitive Health, Education, and Human Services* by K.M McInnis, H.E. Petracchi, and M. Morgenbesser. Appendix B provides resources to help with evaluation and resources for getting to know more about the Hmong.

The Hmong Language

The Hmong language is a Sino-Tibetan language. It is one in a family of languages that is characterized by its tonal nature. The Hmong language uses eight general tones. A language tone is a change in pitch and intonation that changes word meaning. While sentence meaning is carried in written English by punctuation and orally by intonation, in oral Hmong, it is often carried by particles at the end of sentences. Hmong words are monosyllabic, consisting of an initial sound followed by a vowel and one of eight tones; there are no final consonant sounds other than [ng]; strictly speaking, there are no compound words.

It is believed that, until the middle of the twentieth century, Hmong was an oral language. In the early 1950s, several missionaries to the tribe peoples of Indochina, with the assistance of informants, began to write the Hmong language using what they termed the Romanized Popular Alphabet—Laos, ca. 1957 (RPA). It must be noted that the writers, using the RPA, arbitrarily selected written Roman alphabet symbols to represent the oral tones at the end of written Hmong words. That final written alphabet symbol is simply the tonal marker, it is never articulated as a phoneme (Yang, 1993). For example, [liab], the Hmong word for red, is pronounced [lia] not [liab]. More information on these tonal markers is included later in the section on the Hmong alphabet.

Hmong word order is generally the same as English, subject-verb-object. Complex and compound sentences are constructed in ways similar to English. However, the Hmong language has many differences from English. For example, questions are formed by adding question words within the sentence rather than by intonation or by changing word order. There is no gender change with nouns and adjectives. Nouns are divided into classes similar to genders, but based on categories other than sex. Unlike English, adjectives and other modifiers follow rather than precede nouns; verbs are not inflected. There are three groups of pronouns: singular, dual, and plural. Among the particles are: classifiers, question indictors, tense and voice indicators, and pre-verbal and post-verbal intensifiers. Hmong oral language may or may not have a subject, several verbs, liberal use of dialogue, and much replication of structure. Single verb construction allows a single subject to combine with more than one verb to form a single clause. The extended language contains four-word idioms, metaphors, riddles, song-chants, musical instruments [the mouth harp and the qeej], ceremonial and ritual language, ceremonial and ritual chants, and seven-meter poetry (Yang, 1993). For comparisons between the English and Hmong langugaes, see Appendix C.

Sound System of Hmong

The following information is reprinted and adapted from Cheng's *Assessing Asian Language Performance: Guidelines for Evaluating Limited-English Proficient Students.*
- Several consonant sounds, such as /p/, /t/, /r/, /qh/, /ts/, and /t/, have both aspirated and unaspirated forms.
- /r/ is a stop rather than a liquid.
- Tongue placement is approximately midplate.
- Aspirated /r/ may sound like English /t/, while unaspirated /r/ may sound like English /d/.
- In Hmong, [ng] is the only final consonant sound. Consonant clusters, which occur only in initial positions, include nasals plus stops (for example, /np/, /nt/, and /nts/ and nasals plus stops plus /e/ (for example, /npl/)].
- No vowels are reduced to schwa.
- Word meaning changes with tonal marker shifts.

The phonemic characteristics of the Hmong language may create certain difficulties for Hmong who are trying to learn English, Cheng suggests. For example, English consonant clusters may be difficult for a speaker of Hmong to pronounce. Because there are no final consonants in Hmong, other than [ng], many may tend to drop final English consonants. In addition to phonemic differences, there are many morphological differences between Hmong and English. For example, noun plurals and noun possessives do not exist in Hmong, there is no apostrophe [s], there is no [-s] to denote third person singular form, and verb tense changes by adding a word before the verb rather than an inflection to the word itself.

The Hmong Alphabet—Tsaj Ntawv Moob

The Hmong alphabet is written here in the RPA.

Single Consonants—Cov Tsaj Ntawv Txiv Ib Tug
c d** h k l m n p q r s t v x y z

Double Consonant Combination—Cov Tsaj Ntawv Txiv Txooj Ob Tug
ch dl* hl hm** hn** kh ml nc ng nk npnq nr nt ny ph pl qh rh th ts tx xy

Triple consonant combinations—Cov Tsaj Ntawv Txiv Txooj Peb Tug
dln* hml** hny** nch* ndl nkh nph npl nqh nrh nth nts ntx plh tsh txh

Quadruple Consonant Combination—Cov Tsaj Ntawv Txiv Txooj Plaub Tug
ndlh* nplh ntsh ntxh

Single Vowels—Cov Tsaj Ntawv Nam
a e i o u w

Double Vowels—Cov Tsaj Ntawv Nam Txooj Ob Tug
aa* ai au aw ee ia** oo ua

*Hmong Leng (Green Hmong) only
**Hmong Dawb (White Hmong) only

Tonal Markers—Cov Dim (Muaj Cim Lub Suab

The original writers of Hmong chose the following RPA alphabet characters to represent the eight tones of Hmong. They appear in written Hmong at the end of each word, but are simply tonal markers, not to be confused with English sounds.

Tone	RPA Character	Written Sample
High	b	cim sab (siab)
High-falling	j	cim ntuj
Mid-rising	v	cim txiv (kuv)
Mid	*	cim ua (tsi sau dlaab tsi le)
Low	s	cim has (mus)
Low breathing	g	cim neeg
Short low	m	cim nam (niam)
Low-mid	d	cim tod

* No RPA character was assigned to indicate the mid or neutral tone. Therefore, when written, the word will end with a vowel character with no consonant character indicating the mid tone.

Hmong pronunciation, standard English pronunciation, and RPA graphemic representations also vary. For example, Xia is pronounced [sia] not [zia], Soua is pronounced [shooa] not [sooa], Yang is pronounced both [ja] and [jang], lub paj ntaub. Hmong needlework (flower cloth) is both pronounced [pa ntwo] and [pan dow]. To learn the Hmong language, a person should work with a native or proficient bilingual speaker. In addition to the variations described here, the tone determines word meaning in Hmong, and a person may innocently say something embarrassing, or worse, insulting to a native speaker.

Conclusion

In summary, speech and language pathologists must understand their own culture and the impact it brings to their practice whether in diagnosis or therapy. Speech and language pathologists then must try to understand students' behavior by viewing their behaviors from their own cultural contexts (Jackson, F., 1995). Breakdown in communication occurs when the conversational participants make false assumptions about each other's knowledge and experience (Cheng, L.L, 1996).

This chapter has attempted to give the necessary information on history, culture, and dialect or second language differences to prepare the speech and language pathologist for the next step—assessment.

References

Berry, J.W. *Human Ecology and Cognitive Style: Comparative Studies in Cultural and Psychological Adaptation*. New York: Sage/Halstead, 1976.

Bliatou, Thowpaou, et al. *Handbook for Teaching Hmong-Speaking Students*. Folsom, CA: Folsom Cordova Unified School District, 1988.

Bruner, Jerome. *Acts of Meaning*. Cambridge, MA: Harvard University Press, 1990.

Canale, Michael. "On Some Theoretical Framework for Language Proficiency." In *Language Proficiency and Academic Achievement*. Ed. C. Rivera. Clevedon, England: Multilingual Matters, Ltd., 1984.

Cheng, L.L. *Assessing Asian Language Performance: Guidelines for Evaluating Limited-English Proficient Students*. Oceanside, CA: Academic Communication Associates, 1991.

Cheng, L.L. "Beyond Bilingualism: A Quest for Communicative Competence." *Topics of Language Disorders* 16.4, pp. 9-21.

Collier, J.J., and C. Collier. "Referring Culturally Different Children: Sociocultural Considerations." *Academic Therapy* 20.4, pp. 503-509.

Crago, M.B., and Cole, Michael. "Using Ethnography to bring Children's Communicative and Cultural Words in Focus." In *Pragmatics of Language: Clinical Practical Issues*. Ed. Gallagher, T. San Diego, CA: Singular Publishing Group, 1991.

Cummins, J. "The Role of Primary Language Development in Promoting Educational Success for Language Minority Students." In *Schooling and Language Minority Students: A Theoretical Framework*. Los Angeles, CA: Evaluation, Dissemination, and Assessment Center, 1981.

Cummins, J. *Bilingualism and Special Education: Issues in Assessment and Pedagogy*. Clevedon, England: Multicultural Matters, Ltd., 1984.

Damico, J.S., and E.V. Hamayan. *Multicultural Language Intervention: Addressing Cultural and Linguistic Diversity*. Buffalo, NY: Educom Associates Inc., 1992.

Dillard, J.L. *Black English: Its History and Usage in the United States*. New York: Seabury Press, 1972

Erickson, Joan. "Communicative Disorders in Multicultural Populations." Presentation to Wisconsin Speech Language Hearing Association Convention, May 1993.

Gill, W. *Issues in African American Education*. Nashville, TN: Horn Publisher and Imprint of Winston-Derek Publishers, 1991.

Grant, Gloria, ed. *In Praise of Diversity*. Omaha, NE: Center for Urban Education, 1977.

Hale-Benson, J.E. *Black Children: Their Roots, Cultural and Learning Style*. Baltimore, MD: Johns Hopkins University Press, 1982.

Hymes, D. "What is Ethnography?" In *Children in and out of School: Ethnography and Education*. Eds. P. Gilmore and A. Glatthorn. Washington, DC: Center for Applied Linguistics, 1982.

Jackson, Francesina. "Educating a Diverse Learner Community." Presentation to Wausau School District, August 1995.

Krashen, S. *Principles and Practice in Second Language Acquisition*. New York: Pergammon Press, 1982.

Lo, Choua, personal interview, 1994.

McInnis, K.M., H.E. Petracchi, and M. Morgenbesser. *The Hmong in America: Providing Ethnic-Sensitive Health, Education and Human Services*. Dubuque, Iowa: Kendall Hunt, 1990.

Morrow, R.D. "What's in a Name: In Particular a Southeast Asian Name?" *Young Children*, September 1989.

Nazzaro, J.N., ed, *Culturally Diverse Exceptional Children*, Reston, VA: Council for Exceptional Children, 1981

Owens, R.E. *Language Development: An Introduction*. New York: Macmillin Publishing Co, 1991.

Padilla, A., ed. *Acculturation: Theory, Models, and Some New Findings*. American Association for the Advancement of Science: Symposium Series, No. 39. Boulder, CO: Westview Press, 1980.

Scott, Diane. American Speech-Language-Hearing Association Multicultural Affairs Dept., personal interview, 1995.

Skutnabb-Kangas, Tove, and P. Toukomas. *Language in the Process of Cultural Assimilation and Structural Incorporation of Linguistic Minorities*. Arlington, VA: National Clearinghouse for Bilngual Education, 1979.

Taylor, Orlando. *Treatment of Communication Disorders in Culturally and Linguistically Diverse Populations*. San Diego, CA: College Hill Press, 1986.

Taylor, Orlando. "Pragmatic Considerations in Addressing Race, Ethnicity, and Cultural Diversity Within the Academy." In *Multicultural Literacy in Communication Disorders: A Manual for Teaching Cultural Diversity within the Professional Education Curriculum*. Ed. L. Cole. Rockville, MD: American Speech-Language-Hearing Association, 1990.

Wisconsin Department of Public Instruction. *Language Sample Analysis: The Wisconsin Guide*. Madison, WI: Department of Public Instruction, 1992.

Wolfram, W. *Dialects and American English*. Englewood Cliffs, NJ: Prentice Hall, 1991.

Xiong, William, personal interview, 1994.

Yang, Dao. *Hmong at the Turning Point*. Minneapolis, MN: WorldBridge Associates, Ltd., 1993

Web Sites

Netnoir: An outlet for information on sports, education, music, and business. Available on America Online (http://www.netnoir@aol.com).

The Universal Black Pages: An in-depth resource of African American home pages with numerous links to other sites (http://www.gatech.edulbgsal).

Asian American Web Site: The site includes Web indexes such as ChinaScape that discusses news, people, literature, and the arts. It also links to other sites (http://www.ugcs.caltech.edul).

3

Assessment

Introduction

Assessment of language skills, while always challenging, is particularly difficult when the diagnostician must determine if a particular communication behavior results from a communication disorder, a social dialect, English as a second language, or a combination of these. Based on research findings and clinical experiences, language development as a discipline has changed, and assessment practices have shifted to reflect these changes.

In the 1950s, language focused on vocabulary and articulation. In the 1960s, the focus moved to syntax; and in the 1970s researchers' attention shifted to semantics and phonology. The study of pragmatics in the 1980s laid the groundwork for an emphasis on discourse in the 1990s (Westby and Erickson, 1992). Thus, it is only recently that language theories considered the "whole"—functional use of language—rather than its discrete aspects.

Current beliefs about language suggest that it is more than the sum of its components. Mastery of phonology, syntax, morphology, and pragmatics does not necessarily mean that a student can integrate all of these parts into meaningful communication. Oral and written language are now viewed as integrated parts of normal language development, which are interdependent. As more of the children in their classrooms come from non-English speaking and various cultural backgrounds, educators have begun to celebrate student diversity rather than student homogeneity.

Speech and language pathologists have responded by shifting their assessment strategies from standardized testing or other quantitative methods that measure discrete units of language semantics, syntax, or phonology to more integrative and qualitative methods that provide a rich description of the student's communicative competencies. Cultural and social factors that support or inhibit a student's performance on literacy tasks are considered part of the diagnostic picture and add to interpretation of the descriptions gathered. These changes in assessment strategies positively contribute to the task of sorting language differences from language disorders.

The Role of Standardized Testing

Educational literature is replete with comments critical of using standardized tests with students who are from linguistically and culturally diverse backgrounds. The following comments made at least ten years ago by experts in the field of speech pathology still hold true.

"At present, there are no standardized assessment procedures that provide a valid evaluation of language disorders in speakers whose native language is not standard English" (Taylor, Payne, and Anderson, 1983).

"Given the present state of the art in speech and language tests, it can be concluded that there are few, if any, standardized measures that can provide a completely valid and nonbiased evaluation of handicapping conditions for linguistically and culturally diverse populations" (Taylor and Payne, 1986).

"Black children are often misevaluated, owing to the inability of these measures to differentiate between language differences and language disorders" (Taylor and Peters-Johnson, 1986).

Clearly, using standardized assessment tools with students from linguistically and culturally diverse backgrounds raises concerns.

Why are Standardized Tests Discriminatory?

Most tests are normed on a majority population (Anglo) that speaks Standard American English dialect. Few standardized tests have been designed for children that speak non-mainstream English dialects.

Even when tests have included minorities in the standardization sample, the numbers have tended to be small and not representative of the whole population. Averaging the responses of a small number or a small percentage of students who are linguistically and culturally diverse into the larger sample group obscures whatever differences may exist.

Test content generally reflects middle-class Euro-American experiences. Using tests with students who do not closely match the description of the standardization sample and whose culture does not reflect typical Euro-American experiences can result in cultural bias. For example, illustrations used to elicit a response in a test might depict situations that are not within the realm of experiences of urban, minority children. Items on the Peabody Picture Vocabulary Test-revised (PPVT-R) include tractor, forest, bark, reel, vine, balcony. Items on the Elicited One Word Picture Vocabulary Test-Revised (EOWPVT-R) include typewriter, suitcases, tractor, helicopter, anchor. Educators must consider that the experiential background of some students do not include such concepts or vocabulary. "Most standardized tests are culturally biased for any group whose sociocultural background differs from that of the group whom the norms were established" (Erickson and Omark, 1981, p. 126).

Tests typically measure mastery of Standard American English. As such, they are of questionable use in identifying disorders in students whose primary mode of communication differs from standard English. The linguistic content of the test may not be appropriate for children who have not been exposed to the content of the test.

Most standardized tests reflect a discrete-point approach to language assessment. That is, they measure discrete aspects of language, such as vocabulary, grammar, syntax, and phonology. Discrete-point tests are more affected by linguistic or cultural differences than are other assessment strategies.

Educators tend to overrate the value of standardized test scores. This tendency results in the increased likelihood of misuse in the evaluation of children from linguistically and culturally diverse backgrounds.

Children who are unfamiliar with a "testing framework" or "testing situation" used in standardized tests may be at a disadvantage. The situation itself may be threatening or foreign to the cognitive styles of students from linquistically or culturally diverse backgrounds. Results that accrue from the tests are therefore questionable.

How to decrease the discriminatory effects of standardized tests

Using standardized tests with students from linguistically and culturally diverse backgrounds has many drawbacks. Some critics have suggested alternatives to standardized tests, but not all writers are in agreement. Frequently mentioned alternatives and their limitations are listed below. Note that none of these solutions is a good alternative for the practicing speech and language pathologist who must make decisions about a student's need for special education because of a language disorder.

Develop new tests appropriate to the linguistic and cultural background of the students to be tested. This strategy ensures that the test content will be relevant. However, it is time consuming and costly, if not impossible, to construct specific tests for each cultural group.

Modify existing tests for local use by adapting test content to reflect more culturally valid content. Modifying a test in this way may result in an instrument that has greater validity for use in a given school district; however, it is not an easy solution. If the content is changed, new norms must be developed because the published norms will be invalid. Test items may still be linguistically or culturally inappropriate for some segments of a school district's population.

Develop local norms for an existing test by administering the test to a representative sample drawn from the local school district. The resulting norms will be appropriate to the particular population. However, the content validity of the test is not addressed, so that the use of the test may still be invalid. The cost-effectiveness of such an effort may be poor and the resulting "ethnic norms" may be socially dangerous and inappropriate (for example, establishing higher or lower norms for a particular ethnic group might lead to higher or lower expectations for that group).

Translate existing English language tests into the primary language of the student. This can be accomplished by an interpreter or translator of the student's primary language. This strategy should be used only if the interpreter has been trained in test administration procedures and will avoid prompting or interpretation of the student's responses. However, the conditions under which the test was standardized have been violated, and it will not be appropriate to make educational placement decisions based on the test score. If the SLP reports the score, content validity in terms of linguistic or cultural appropriateness of test items remains unresolved. See Appendix D for guidelines for training and using interpreters and translators.

Refrain from using standardized tests entirely. This position has been advanced by some professionals in speech and language as well as related disciplines. This solution dramatizes the crisis that exists with respect to the use of standardized tests; however, it does not offer a viable alternative to the practicing clinician who must complete evaluations and needs valid and reliable assessment tools that will contribute to a non-discriminatory assessment.

Despite these limitations, standardized tests may be used with other assessment strategies to assist in identification of communication delays and disorders if the SLP carefully implements strategies for reducing the likelihood that the use of such tests will result in discrimination or misidentification of students with language disabilities. Speech and language pathologists must consider test selection, administration, and interpretation.

Test Selection

Based on a careful reading of the examiner's manual, a review of the test format, and an examination of individual test items, the speech and language pathologist must select appropriate tests.

Appendixes E, F, and G provide formats for reviewing tests and their content. The Test Evaluation Form (Appendix E) is useful when reading the test manual and reviewing the appropriateness of a test for a specific student. The Checklist for Determination of Potential Discrimination of an Assessment Instrument (Appendix F) and the Evaluation of Discrete-Point Test Form (Appendix G) are helpful when evaluating test content.

Reviewing published tests in such a manner is a time-consuming endeavor but will result in heightened awareness of the potential discriminatory impact of a specific test. Test selection should be made based on the greatest number of quality items found in which common features occur in both standard English and the child's primary language or dialect.

Test Administration

Diagnosticians should administer standardized tests according to the directions in the manual; however, they must be sensitive to the student's culture, interaction style, and reaction to the testing situation. Otherwise, it may be difficult to establish rapport with the student and interpret responses.

Evaluators also must consider the student's experience with the testing situation. Every test response must be learned. It should not be assumed that the student can respond in the manner required by the test, and testing should not begin until the student understands the task expectations. The evaluator should allow the student to practice on the types of items and activities included in the test to ensure that the student understands the instructions and the kinds of responses expected. The evaluator also should demonstrate the nature of the response expected and provide examples of the types of responses that will receive maximum credit. Because it is inappropriate to use actual test items, similar items and materials for practice activities will need to be developed. Time spent preparing the student for the types of tasks that will be encountered on the test will increase the probability of valid test results.

If translations of test instructions or activities are necessary, an interpreter should give the test. The interpreter must understand the rationale, procedures, and information desired. The translation need not be literal, but it should include idiomatic expressions of the intent of the test or activity. A person from the same ethnic group as the student should give the translation. The test examiner should not attempt to give the test while the interpreter translates; this confuses the student.

Test Interpretation

Speech and language pathologists must be sensitive to the limitations of tests and use caution when interpreting test results to identify a student from a linguistically and culturally diverse background as having a language disorder. If standardized tests are used, the SLP must carefully interpret the results.

Test scores should not be used as the sole basis for identification of a language disorder.

Speech and language pathologists should never base eligibility decisions solely on a test score or the results of a single instrument. This is particularly true when tests are used with students from linguistically and culturally diverse backgrounds. Because low scores may result from various factors, the speech and language pathologist must consider possible reasons for the student's performance. Errors that are not typical of other children with similar linguistic and cultural backgrounds may be evidence of a possible disorder. Standardized test results must always be compared with data derived from other measures.

Use test results in conjunction with information obtained from samples of language use in natural settings.

Standardized tests may provide information about possible problems that can be better identified in natural communication. Further assessment through language sampling or other descriptive assessment strategies can corroborate test results and help the speech and language pathologist determine if there are problems in the child's functional use of language. "A child should be considered to have a communicative disorder only if evidence of a deficit is found during conversational speech" (Mattes and Omark, 1984, p. 70).

The extent to which test performance is influenced by cultural and environmental factors unique to the individual being assessed needs to be explored.

Two children from the same cultural background may differ in terms of values, customs, and beliefs related to their culture. Each child is unique, and therefore, must be viewed as such in the interpretation of test data. Reviewing test results with the child's parents and/or guardians can provide information about cultural and environmental factors that may have affected performance. Using multiple informants further reduces possible bias.

In *Interpretation and Translation in Bilingual B.A.S.E.*, Gloria Toliver-Weddington and Joan Erickson provide the following suggestions for using standardized tests with students from linguistically and culturally diverse backgrounds. Speech and language pathologists should implement these strategies with caution, tailoring them to the specific student and to the reasons for completing the assessment using standardized testing measures.

● Select a test that has the most valid items for the skills to be assessed.
● Examine the directions and each of the test items in order to determine whether the minority child to be assessed has had access to the information.
● Develop a list of alternative directions and responses to items before administering the test.
● Administer the test as recommended in the examiner's manual first. Because the directions are not usually a test item, reword immediately if indicated. (Note: translations of directions into the student's primary language and practice responding to the type of tasks

and providing the type of responses included in the test are also recommended by some authors.)

● The examiner may need to make the following procedural modifications to obtain a more accurate description of the child's communication

—Provide additional time for the child to respond.

—Continue the test even though a basal is not established.

—Continue the test beyond the ceiling.

—Ask the child to name the picture or point to actual objects for items missed on a task that uses pictures for assessing comprehension.

—Encourage the child to explain choices that are incorrect according to the scoring guidelines.

● Record all of the student's responses. When a student changes an answer, give him or her credit, especially when the student demonstrates that he or she knows the correct answer.

● Compare the child's responses with the ones considered to be correct on the test. For responses that are the same or similar, mark them correct.

● For those items that are incorrect according to the test manual, compare the child's answers with reported features of the child's native language or dialect and rescore when appropriate.

● Score the test in two ways. First, record scores as indicated in the examiner's manual even though the directions may have been changed. Next, rescore each item, allowing credit for those items that are considered correct in the child's language system and/or experience.

● Compare both sets of scores with the norms. Typically, the adjusted scores are higher than the unadjusted scores; however, children with communication disorders will achieve low scores no matter how the test is scored.

● When reporting test results, indicate that adjustments have been made. The evaluator should describe the items that were modified, what was done to modify test procedures, and the differences in the child's responses after the modification.

● Focus on what a student can do rather than what a child cannot do; look for what a child knows as well as what a child does not know.

Alternative Assessment Strategies

Given the inadequacy of standardized assessment measures, speech and language pathologists need to identify and use alternative assessment strategies to more appropriately determine the presence of a language disorder or difference. The following alternatives to standardized tests will assist in this process.

Use criterion-referenced tasks when assessing the language of students from linguistically and culturally diverse backgrounds. Orlando Taylor and K.T. Payne recommend this nonstandardized approach as an alternative to inappropriate use of standardized tests. Criterion-referenced measures offer no scientific developmental sequence data. Therefore, specific linguistic behaviors (the criterion) must be identified before the student begins the test. Although data collected through criterion-referenced assessment is not intended to compare students' performance, it does link evaluation to instructional goals (Vaughn-Cooke, 1983). Grade-level expectations in regular education and report cards that reflect the student's progress in meeting those expectations are ways to use criterion-referenced assessment.

Use language sample analysis (LSA) when assessing the language of students from linguistically and culturally diverse backgrounds. A language sample is a collection of spontaneous utterances taken for the purpose of examining the student's language proficiency in a more spontaneous and functional conversation context. It allows a comparison between formal test results and functional language used in the context of a specific speech community. Spontaneous language production allows the student to demonstrate the true range of his or her language abilities as he or she communicates a variety of messages in either his or her first or second language or dialect (Wisconsin Department of Public Instruction, 1992). A language sample can be used to document growth and development of language proficiency and can be helpful in corroborating or refuting discrete-point test results. When appropriate developmental information is available, LSA enables the speech and language pathologist to compare the student's performance to that of his or her peers (for example, Developmental Sentence Scoring). Language sample analysis is also useful in establishing intervention strategies that are functional and will have immediate results in improving the student's communicative competency. Methods of LSA are described in detail in *Language Sample Analysis: The Wisconsin Guide* (Wisconsin Department of Public Instruction, 1992). Application of language sample analysis strategies with typically developing African American and Hmong students are summarized in Chapter 4 of this guide. The case studies in Chapter 6 may provide further insight into how LSA can be used in conjunction with other assessment strategies to differentiate language differences from language disorders.

Use other descriptive assessment strategies in conjunction with standardized assessment tools. E.V. Hamayan and J.S. Damico (1991) state that language and communication "should be treated as dynamic, synergistic, and integrative with both intrinsic cognitive factors and extrinsic contextual features." Incorporating such a view of communication into assessment practices can help limit the bias inherent in the assessment of students from linguistically and culturally diverse backgrounds and assist in differentiating language disorders from language differences. This becomes increasingly important as U.S. demographics change. By the year 2000, one-third of the people in the United States will be from minority groups with many from homes where English is not the primary language (Westby, 1992). Descriptive or qualitative assessment strategies differ significantly from quantitative or discrete-point assessment strategies in several important ways. The characteristics of both qualitative and quantitative assessment methods based on the work of M. Patton and C. Westby (1992) are contrasted in Figure 11.

 Figure 11

Characteristics of Qualitative and Quantitative Assessment Strategies

Qualitative Strategy	Quantitative Strategy
Study of real-world situations as they occur naturally	Study of behavior in experimentally controlled situations
Insider-direct contact and personal experiences and insights are important parts of the inquiry and critical to understanding	Outsider; applies statistical analysis to objective data
Focus on the whole individual and cultural values	Focus on isolated variables and cause-effect relationships
Attention to process; reality viewed as a dynamic, changing system	Attention to product; reality viewed as unchanging facts
Each case is viewed as special and unique	Subjects viewed collectively as a group with special characteristics
Evaluator includes personal experience and empathetic insight as relevant data	Evaluator uses objective tests

---

Ethnography as a Descriptive Assessment Tool

Ethnography is a qualitative method of investigation. It has its roots in anthropology and is sometimes called an anthropological field study approach. It is the "process of interpreting culture (ethno-) in writing (-graphy) from the native point of view" (Kovarsky, 1992). Ethnography is a systematic, scientific process for understanding behaviors by studying them in multiple contexts. W.R. Borg and M.D. Gall (1983) list four principle tenets of the ethnographic approach.

● Phenomenology: the clinician/researcher adopts the perspective of the student being assessed.

● Holism: context is viewed as essential for understanding the behaviors being observed.

● Nonjudgmentalism: emphasis is on observing or recording a total situation without judgment or bias. After obtaining detailed notes, a hypothesis can be generated in an attempt to understand the behavior being observed.

● Contextualization: data need to be interpreted in the context of the situation in which it was gathered.

Ethnographic methods of assessment offer a powerful alternative or supplementary means of examining the communication skills of students. It has a long history of use in understanding variations in communication patterns and interaction rules in linguistically and culturally diverse groups. An ethnographic approach to assessment provides more detailed descriptions of behavior. As a result, there is an increased chance that the data represent the student's typical skills. Data interpretation is less biased and more valid because it is interpreted through the world view or perspective of the student's culture. Finally, intervention goals have a better chance of generalizing to the real world because data collection is based upon the environments in which the student is expected to communicate.

Whenever there is reliance on multiple informants and interactants in data collection, possible bias in the assessment of students is reduced. Figure 12 lists the kinds of information a diagnostician might gather using multiple sources of information.

■ **Figure 12**

Possible Sources of Information and Their Purpose

(Adapted from *Assessing Asian Language Performance: Guidelines for Evaluating Limited English-Proficient Students* by L.L. Cheng. Oceanside, CA: Academic Communication Associates, 1991.)

Informant	Function
Older sibling	Provide language model and comment on the child's language use
Parents	Comment on the child's language at home and in comparison to that of siblings
Monolingual or monodialectical peers	Comment on interaction
Monolingual or monodialectical teachers	Comment on the overall behavior, academic skills, learning style, learning rate, attention
Bilingual upper grade schoolmate or upper grade schoolmate using the same dialect	Comment on native language fluency or fluency using the dialect and provide articulation and language model
Bilingual teacher or assistant; teacher or assistant from the same cultural background	Comment on language acquisition and competency from the viewpoint of the culture; may conduct assessment or remediation
Linguist	Comment on features of native language or alternative dialect
English as a Second Language teacher	Comment on acquisition of English compared to other children of the same cultural and language background
Foreign students	Comment on the native language of the student
Bilingual psychologist	Provide psychological profile

Lily Cheng (1990) and D.N. Ripich and F.M. Spinelli (1985) recommend several activities in conducting ethnographic assessment:

• Critically examine your own world values, views, beliefs, way of life, communicative style, learning style, cognitive style, and personal biases.

• Describe the child's communication breakdown based on information from multiple sources.

• Interview members of the child's family and work with them to collect data regarding the child and the home environment.

• Consult with the classroom teachers and aides.

• Employ procedures designed to describe the student's linguistic behavior in natural settings.

• Summarize observations and identify patterns of communication, taking care to validate observations by comparing information from multiple perspectives.

Using ethnographic procedures in a school setting is not without its difficulties. Ripich and Spinelli suggest that limited physical and psychological access to the classroom environment is a major barrier in some schools because access is not easily granted by teachers and administrators. Teachers may perceive that the observer is judging them or their curriculum rather than attempting to gain a better understanding of the linguistic and discourse demands of the classroom environment. The child may be wary of being observed and may not interact in typical ways with an observer present.

The speech and language pathologist may be unaware of his or her own bias and preconceptions that affect interpretation of the behaviors and interactions observed. Also, some school districts require the use of standardized tests for program placement. Speech and language staff members may not have had training in the use of descriptive assessment strategies, and standardized tests are familiar and easily accessible. Standardized tests may also be more quickly administered when large caseloads limit the time available for diagnostic activities.

Distinguishing Language Differences from Language Disorders

Federal and state policies require that school districts document the modifications attempted in regular education curriculum and/or instruction that might allow student success when considering if there is a need for referral to exceptional education. These types of interventions can be completed by any member of the educational team who may be interacting with the student: bilingual/English as a Second Language specialists, classroom teachers, psychologists, nurses, family members, members of the student's cultural community, social workers, and so forth. When a collaborative team approach to problem solving is used, the likelihood of bias decreases. For many students, this level of intervention will be sufficient to ensure learning success.

The process can include a variety of strategies tailored to the individual student, his or her learning difficulties, and the setting. As Figure 13 suggests, the process begins with careful identification of the teacher's and/or parents' concerns. As these concerns are described, information about the student's cultural, social, experiential, and linguistic background can be gathered. While cultural patterns influence the way a person perceives, organizes, processes, and utilizes information, family values, beliefs, strengths, and needs will vary within cultural groups. Assumptions about a student based on race alone will be invalid.

Information gathered about a student is compared and contrasted to the cultural, social, and linguistic environments in which the student is expected to function. A careful analysis can help to identify inherent similarities and differences. At the same time, information about the student's learning style, motivation, interests, and strengths can be gathered and compared to the teacher's instructional style, curriculum content, and requirements.

A Model of Assessment to Assist in Distinguishing Language Differences from Language Disorders

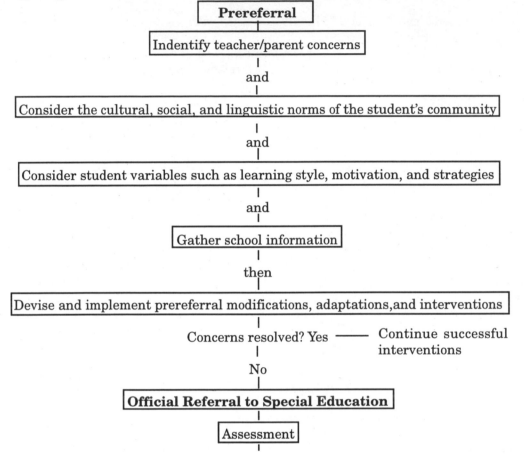

Prereferral

Indentify teacher/parent concerns

and

Consider the cultural, social, and linguistic norms of the student's community

and

Consider student variables such as learning style, motivation, and strategies

and

Gather school information

then

Devise and implement prereferral modifications, adaptations,and interventions

Concerns resolved? Yes ——— Continue successful interventions

No

Official Referral to Special Education

Assessment

Key points for LCD students:
- Assessment must be multifaceted and multidimensional
- Observations and interviews must be used to obtain assessment information
- Assessment must be conducted in the child's native language and/or results obtained interpreted in light of the student's native language or dialect
- Traditional tests have a limited role in LCD assessments

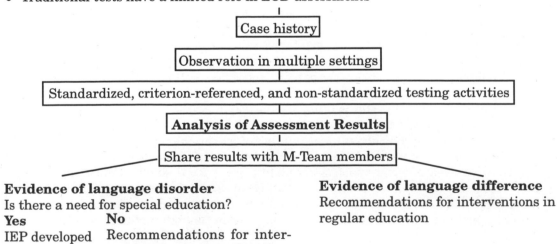

Case history

Observation in multiple settings

Standardized, criterion-referenced, and non-standardized testing activities

Analysis of Assessment Results

Share results with M-Team members

Evidence of language disorder
Is there a need for special education?
Yes   **No**
IEP developed   Recommendations for inter-
                ventions in regular education

Evidence of language difference
Recommendations for interventions in regular education

As these are compared and contrasted, matches and mismatches may be identified. Careful review of the student's educational records will give perspective to the chronicity of the concerns identified as well as overall achievement. Previous interventions that may have been attempted, their effectiveness, and the results of any achievement testing conducted will also be helpful.

When information from all of these sources is combined, the team will be able to form hypotheses about possible modifications and adaptations of the student's program. These modifications may resolve the concerns and eliminate the need for further assessment or intervention.

Appendixes H through M provide various tools to assist in this process. All of these can be used by any member of the educational team working with or observing the student. Duplication and customization of these forms to meet the needs of specific environments or staff members are encouraged. The process uses the strategies of observation, records review, interview, and collaboration. General education staff members are responsible for implementation of the suggested adaptations or modifications that result from this collaborative process. Thus, it is imperative that these educators be part of the information-gathering and problem-solving activities.

Official Referral to Special Education

If the modifications and adaptations identified through this process are not successful in resolving the initial concerns, and the team suspects that the student may have one or more disabilities that will require special education, a referral to exceptional education may be made. The referral initiates an assessment by a multidisciplinary team (M-team). The process of referral through an M-team assessment, development of an individualized education program (IEP), and placement in special education is defined and regulated by state and federal law and local school district policy. The following suggestions facilitate the task of distinguishing a language disorder from a language difference in the context of completing the M-team assessment.

Once team members have decided to refer a student for exceptional education consideration, parental notice and consent must occur prior to the initiation of any additional assessment activities. The previous activities that occurred and their effectiveness should be reported as part of the referral. They help substantiate the reasons for suspecting that the student has a disability.

When consent for the evaluation has been obtained from the student's parent(s), the next step in the process, the M-team assessment, may begin. Assessment activities are always tailored to the referral concerns identified. However, some issues are common to the assessment of any student from a linguistically and culturally diverse background.

Assessment must be multifaceted and multidimensional. In other words, a variety of sources of information must be used. The use of descriptive techniques and strategies borrowed from ethnographic field studies will ensure that characteristics of the student's cultural background and home are considered. Descriptive techniques that use samples of language use for functional tasks as measures of communicative competency will ensure that the student's language is viewed as more than isolated abilities in semantics, syntax, morphology, and phonology.

Observations and interviews must be used to obtain assessment information. Because discrete-point testing strategies are so vulnerable to cultural bias, assessment of the student's language skills should be augmented in as many other ways as possible.

Careful interview of parents or others who are from the student's cultural community and are familiar with the student is essential. The interviewer must convey respect and interest in what the parent is saying and how it is being stated. Feedback messages may not always be clear: a lack of eye contact and or verbal responses may be a sign of both respect and a lack of understanding. Be aware of cultural differences in interpreting interactions.

Select the location of the interview and observation with care. The home may provide the most comfortable and natural setting. Use a variety of questions: general descriptive ("tell me about..."), specific ("tell me what you did when..."), and guided ("describe..."). Ask only one question at a time, and be sensitive to the need to probe for more information. Listening to and observing the parents or other representatives of the student's culture speak and interact will give the speech and language pathologist valuable information about the language and communication style of the home.

Appendixes N and O provide sample interview and observation forms that can be used as part of various assessment activities. Remember that multiple informants and multiple sources of information will assist the M-team in minimizing or eliminating possible bias.

Assessment activities must be conducted in the student's native language and/or the results must be interpreted in view of the student's native language or dialect. It may not always be feasible to conduct the assessment in the student's primary language. It is, however, always possible to gather information about the student's linguistic and cultural background and interpret results from assessments conducted in Standard American English in view of that information. Members of the student's cultural community should be used to define and corroborate the communication difficulties. Failure to do this may result in inappropriate identification of language disorders.

While standardized tests may be most easily obtained and even required for identification of students with exceptional educational needs, their use with students from linguistically and culturally diverse backgrounds is questionable. If they are used, extreme care must be used in selecting the test and in interpreting and reporting results. An analysis of the error patterns must be made in view of the student's primary language or dialect. In any case, the role of standardized tests should be limited, and standardized tests should never be the sole assessment strategy employed. See Appendixes E and F for tools to assist the evaluator in selection of standardized assessment tools.

Information from multiple informants includes a complete case history and background and school information that will assist the diagnostician in determining language dominance, proficiency, and preference as well as the use of dialect. Sociolinguistic competency and proficiency should be assessed in both the student's first language and second language.

Information is collected from the child. Hearing is screened and/or tested (see Appendix P). Observations of language use in multiple settings occur. The teacher and parent(s) can provide information about learning style and achievement. Language samples are collected or probes of language ability are used to elicit targeted language behaviors.

Analysis of Assessment Results

Once all assessment information is gathered, an analysis of the data is conducted as the next step in the process of distinguishing a language disorder from a language difference. Judgments regarding the student's proficiency in English and his or her primary language and the student's language preference contribute to interpretation of other data. The analysis should ensure that the student's performance is representative of his or her typical performance across communication tasks, partners, and environments.

By noting the patterns of performance and then comparing these patterns to characteristics of the student's cultural and linguistic background, features attributed to language differences can be identified. The examiner looks for evidence that the problem is exhibited in both languages and cannot be attributed to assessment bias, cultural interference, normal second-language acquisition, or dialectical phenomenon. Remaining problems that cannot be explained by linguistic or cultural factors may be representative of language disorders and should be shared with the M-team for assistance in determining if these issues interfere with learning and require special education.

References

Borg, W.R., and M.D. Gall. *Educational Research: An Introduction.* 4th ed. White Plains, NY: Longman Inc., 1983.

Cheng, L.L. "The Identification of Communicative Disorders in Asian-Pacific Students." *Journal of Childhood Communicative Disorders* 13.1, pp. 113-119.

Cheng, L.L. *Assessing Asian Language Performance: Guidelines for Evaluating Limited-English Proficient Students.* 2nd ed. Oceanside, CA: Academic Communication Associates, 1991.

Erickson, G., and D.R. Omark. *Communication Assessment of the Bilingual/Bicultural Child: Issues and Guidelines.* Baltimore, MD: University Park Press, 1981.

Hamayan, E.V., and J.S. Damico, eds. *Limiting Bias in the Assessment of Bilingual Students.* Austin, TX: Pro-ed, 1991.

Kovarsky, D. "Ethnography and Language Assessment: Toward the Contextualized Description and Interpretation of Communicative Behavior." In *Best Practices in School Speech-Language Pathology: Descriptive/Nonstandardized Language Assessment.* Eds. W.A. Secord and J.S. Damico. San Antonio, TX: The Psychological Corp., 1992.

Mattes, L.J., and D.R. Omark. *Speech and Language Assessment for the Bilingual Handicapped.* San Diego, CA: College Hill Press, 1984.

Patton, M., and C. Westby. "Ethnography and Research: A Qualitative View" *Topics in Language Disorders* 12(3), 1-14.

Ripich, D.N., and F.M. Spinelli, eds. *School Discourse Problems.* San Diego, CA: College Hill Press, 1985.

Secord, W.A., and J. S. Damico, eds. *Best Practices in School Speech-Language Pathology: Descriptive/Nonstandardized Language Assessment.* San Antonio, TX: The Psychological Corp., 1992.

Taylor, O., and C. Peters-Johnson. "Speech and Language Disorders in Blacks." In *Nature of Communication Disorders in Culturally and Linguistically Diverse Populations.* Ed. O. Taylor. Austin, TX: Pro-ed, 1986.

Taylor, O., and K.T. Payne. "Culturally Valid Testing: A Proactive Approach." In *Nature of Communication Disorders in Culturally and Linguistically Diverse Populations.* Ed. O. Taylor. Austin, TX: Pro-ed, 1986.

Taylor, O., K.T. Payne, and N.B. Anderson. *Distinguishing Between Communication Disorders and Communication Differences.* Washington, DC: Howard University, School of Communications, 1983.

Toliver-Weddington, G., and J. Erickson. "Suggestions for Using Standardized Tests with Minority Children." In *Interpretation and Translation in Bilingual B.A.S.E.* San Diego, CA: Department of Education, 1982.

Vaughn-Cooke, F.B. "Improving Language Assessment in Minority Children." *ASHA* 23.9 (1983).

Westby, C.E. "Ethnographic Interviewing: Asking the Right Questions to the Right People in the Right Ways." *Journal of Childhood Communication Disorders* 13(1), pp. 101-111.

Westby, C.E., and J. Erickson. *Topics in Language Disorders* 13(3), pp. v.-viii.

Wisconsin Department of Public Instruction. *Language Sample Analysis: The Wisconsin Guide.* Madison, WI: Wisconsin Department of Public Instruction, 1992.

4

Language Sample Analysis

African American Subjects
Hmong Subjects
References

Introduction

The goal of Jon Miller's Language Sample Analysis (LSA) research was to determine the cultural relevance of the conversation and narrative sampling conditions for children from different cultural groups who are learning English as a second language. These sampling conditions were developed to provide consistent samples of children's language that were relevant to the communication needs of children through school age.

A method of collecting samples under these standard conditions, transcription, analysis, and interpretation procedures are detailed in *Language Sample Analysis: The Wisconsin Guide* (Wisconsin Department of Public Instruction, 1992). This guide provides a summary of the Reference Database (Miller, 1992) which provides data on 265 children from Wisconsin, 3 to 13 years old, on 25 variables reflecting performance at the semantic and syntactic levels as well as rate, fluency, intelligibility, and errors at the word and utterance level.

In order to document the cultural relevance of the conversation and narrative sampling contexts, language samples were collected from a group of African American students to assess cultural difference and from a group of Hmong students who are learning English as a second language. The Hmong students also provided samples based on a specific story re-telling task using the Frog Story, a picture book without words. The Frog Story provided samples that could be analyzed using detailed story grammar techniques. The Frog Story provides an additional sampling context that can be compared with the standard conversation and narrative contexts.

The analyses of these two sets of language samples is discussed independently, first the African American data set, followed by the Hmong data set. A description of the subjects provides information on age, sex, socio-economic status, and school ability or placement. The selection of both groups was done to insure comparability of factors other than cultural or ethnic group. In some cases, children were excluded from the final analyses. In most cases this was the result of deficiencies in the sampling process: samples were too short (for example, less than 100 complete and intelligible utterances) or the rules for each sample type were not followed (for example, conversation and narrative contexts were mixed).

The variables selected for comparison were those reflecting general developmental progress, for example, mean length of utterance (MLU), number of different words (DW), and total words in the sample (TW); verbal fluency, for example, number of utterances with mazes; and speaking rate, for example, the number of words per minute. These variables provide a broad-based index for comparing the general language skills of African American and Hmong children with the Reference Database to determine if these sampling conditions provide similar opportunities to demonstrate productive language skills.

The procedures followed in identifying the subjects followed those used in developing the Reference Database (RDB) detailed in *LSA: The Wisconsin Guide*. Basically, subjects represented a range of socio-economic status determined by maternal schooling documented by the number of years of school completed, for example, completing high school = 12 and two years of college = 14. The mean socio-economic status was similar for the Hmong, African American, and RDB subject groups. The subject groups had similar numbers of boys and girls in each group. Details regarding the number of subjects in each age or grade grouping can be found in the discussion of the data for each sample.

African American Subjects

Systematic Analysis of Language Transcripts (a computer program designed to analyze language production between two speakers) was performed on each of the conversation and narrative samples produced by the seven- and nine-year-old subjects. The analyses focused on five major variables: MLU, TW, DW as measures of developmental progress; the number of utterances with mazes as an index of word and utterance formulation load; and the number of words produced per minute, an index of speaking rate.

Subjects

The first group of subjects were African American students from the Madison Metropolitan School District and from the Milwaukee Public School District. Language transcripts were analyzed for two groups of students, seven-year-olds and nine-year-olds. The number of analyzable samples from each age group and speaking condition are as follows.

African American Students	7-year-olds	9-year-olds
Conversation	N = 26	N = 27
Narrative	N = 20	N = 30

Results

The African American seven- and nine-year-old subjects performed similarly to the RDB on almost every variable for both the conversation and narrative speaking conditions. Performance was within one standard deviation or better for each of the five variables evaluated. For the seven-year-old subjects, performance was equivalent to the RDB on MLU, TW, and DW for both conversation and narrative samples.

The number of utterances with mazes is similar for the conversation condition, but African American students produce more utterances with mazes in the narrative condition though still within one standard deviation of the mean for the RDB sample. This increase may reflect a style difference or may be a characteristic of this particular group of seven year old children.

The final variable is the number of words produced per minute (WMP), which is a rate measure. The WPM performance is low but within one standard deviation for conversation, and the values are exactly the same for the narrative sampling condition. Because the rate of production was higher in the narrative condition where the child controlled the topic, there may be differences among African American students' ability to interact in conversation with examiners who are white and African American. Comparison with the nine-year-old data provides insight into possible differences in speaking rate among this population.

The conversational data for the nine-year-olds show an interesting trend. The values for MLU, TW, and DW all are above the means for the RDB data though still within one standard deviation. The number of utterances with mazes is high but just below one standard deviation, similar to the younger subjects. The number of words per minute is below the mean but well within one standard deviation of the mean.

The narrative data show scores for TW and DW that are above one standard deviation of the mean for the RDB data, and MLU is very close, 10.38 compared to plus one SD of 10.44 from the RDB data. These numbers suggest the African American children are performing better than 80 percent of the children in the RDB on these measures. This outcome supports a variety of reports that the African American culture is highly verbal. These are the first data from a more formal evaluation of language performance to support this view.

The number of utterances with mazes is more than one standard deviation higher for the narrative samples but not the conversational samples. The nine-year-old data for conversation is similar to that of the seven-year-old subjects in that the means for the African American children are high but still within one SD of the RDB mean. The narrative data suggest that this group of students was less verbally fluent than the RDB sample. A detailed analysis of the nature of the mazes would have to be done to determine if this difference is stylistic (consistent among African American children) or attributable to a few children who have substantial verbal fluency problems.

The final variable to compare is words per minute. The means for both the narrative and conversation samples are within one SD of the mean for the RDB samples. These data suggest that rate of speaking is consistent for the African American children and the children included in the RDB.

The final issue to be discussed for the African American subjects concerns their use of Black Dialect (also known as African American English or Black English). Use of Black Dialect (BD) was coded at the time of transcription based on the BD characteristics found in *LSA: The Wisconsin Guide* (see Appendix A). The codes were inserted at the ends of utterances indicating that all or part of the utterance contained examples of BD. To determine the degree to which BD may be influencing decisions about language performance status, the frequency of dialect use in the conversation and narrative samples for the seven- and nine-year-old subjects was calculated. The following table lists the mean and range of utterances containing examples of BD.

	Conversation		*Narration*	
	Mean	Range	Mean	Range
7-year-olds	15	0 - 45	15	3 - 38
9-year-olds	15	0 - 35	17	2 - 32

This information suggests that dialect use is consistent across speaking conditions and age groups. Several issues about dialect use remain to be examined. Is dialect use a function of the race of the examiner? To what extent is code switching necessary? If a child cannot code switch, is it diagnostic of disordered performance, lack of experience with BD, or lack of experience with standard English? Developing diagnostic criteria for African American children requires addressing these questions in detail in order to distinguish language disorder from language difference.

Summary

These data document that African American children perform similarly on the conversation and narrative language sampling contexts when socio-economic status and ability level are matched with the Reference Database. As African American children get older their language performance exceeds that of the Reference Database children for developmental variables. These data support the characterization of the African American culture as highly verbal.

It is clear from these data that a separate database for African American children is not warranted, and the RDB should be stratified, including the appropriate percentage of African American students representing the population as a whole. Race is not an issue in overall language performance, dialect must be distinguished from disordered performance before diagnosis can be made.

These analyses only evaluate word and utterance level performance and do not cover pragmatic or discourse-level characteristics. The language performance variables evaluated should be considered general indicators of performance status. Diagnosis of a language disorder will require additional analyses of language sample data as well as other tests of language and cognitive abilities.

Hmong Subjects

Systematic Analysis of Language Transcripts (SALT) of language samples from three contexts: conversation, narration (following *LSA: The Wisconsin Guide*), and the Frog Story Retell (see Chapter 5) was undertaken to determine if these sampling conditions provided children learning English as a second language equivalent opportunity to demonstrate their language skills in comparison with children from the mainstream culture.

Subjects

Subjects were students who had completed the English as a Second Language (ESL) Program in their district who were attending second grade or fifth grade. The target was 20 children from each grade. The number of analyzable samples from each grade and speaking condition are as follows.

Hmong Students	*Second Grade*	*Fifth Grade*
Conversation	N = 11	N = 17
Narrative	N = 5	N = 11
Frog	N = 13	N = 17

Results

The first issue concerned the number of samples that could not be included for analysis. While a number of factors contributed to samples being excluded, three reasons accounted for the majority of cases.

First the sample did not meet sampling condition criteria (for example, conversation and narrative conditions were mixed) or children did not appear to be capable of narrative discourse. Few second-grade children produced an acceptable narrative sample. Second, children did not talk long enough (for example, the samples did not contain 100 complete and intelligible utterances). And third, examiners did not follow appropriate sampling procedures (for example, they asked too many questions or used picture books for the narrative condition resulting in the child naming pictures rather than re-telling the story).

If the number of subjects successfully completing each sampling condition is any indication, the narrative condition for the second graders was a more difficult speaking task than conversation or retelling the Frog Story for this group.

SALT was used to analyze the transcripts. Comparisons were made for five major variables: MLU, DW, TW, utterances with mazes, and words per minute, with the relevant age group from the reference database. The second-grade group had a mean age of 8.48 and was compared to the nine-year-old RDB group. The fifth-grade group had a mean age of 11.65 and was compared to the 11-year-old RDB group.

The Hmong student language performance on the three developmental indicators (MLU, DW, and TW) was within one standard deviation of their peers, indicating the general language skills of both the second- and fifth-grade students are comparable to their peers in the RDB. The fact that so few second graders were able to complete the narrative sampling task may mean relating an event or story narrative is particularly difficult for them. They were very successful, however, in retelling the Frog Story, which is a far more structured narrative task. The majority of fifth-grade students were able to perform the SALT narrative task.

Both second- and fifth-grade students produced significantly more mazes than their age-matched peers in both conversation and narrative speaking conditions. This finding will have to be examined in detail to determine its origin and effect on overall communication effectiveness. On the surface, this finding is consistent with second language learners who may produce filled pauses, repetitions, or revisions when searching for the proper word or formulating a unique utterance in the second language. The final variable documented overall speaking rate. The second-grade subjects also talked at a slower rate than their peers, but the fifth graders' rates were the same as their peer group. This may indicate that as age increases, English competence also increases.

Summary

Hmong students who have graduated from ESL programs have a similar grasp of English as their peers on several general measures of language performance. The relatively few number of second-grade subjects that were able to complete the standard narrative task may indicate that performance at the narrative or discourse level is not comparable to their peers. The data also show that speaking rate increases with advancing age, documenting improved verbal facility that may be associated with increased practice. The Frog Story Retell sampling condition appeared to be an easier task judging by the number of successful samples. These samples were shorter overall, resulted in higher MLUs (associated with frequent use of "and then"), and more restricted vocabulary (fewer different words).

How can these data be useful in helping to identify children with specific language impairments when English was their second language? The process of analyzing the three language samples for these children revealed a number of stylistic differences in productive language performance, including:

- excessive use of "and" to initiate utterances
- frequent use of question intonation when non-question utterances resulting in most utterances sounding like questions
- omitting plural /s/ and omitting /s/ on contracted forms
- producing primarily one- and two-word utterances
- very quiet voice
- limited conversational theses
- high frequency of mazes (false starts, repetitions, and reformulations of parts of utterances)
- high frequency of "um" probably reflects searching memory for the proper English word
- responses to questions that are correct syntactically, but not semantically
- generally produce one utterance per topic even on same turn

(Miller, et al, 1990)

Many of these behaviors are likely the result of limited-English proficiency and better English comprehension skills than production skills. For example, the high frequency of mazes may be the result of comprehension monitoring identifying errors in production and attempting to correct them. The Language Sample Analysis methodology provides an opportunity to distinguish performance differences at all linguistic levels: phonological, lexical, syntactic, and pragmatic. Developing appropriate evaluation and interpretation systems for children from linguistically and culturally diverse backgrounds requires description of the cultural background of the family to provide insight into their language production performance.

The data from the Hmong population indicates a central problem in evaluating English proficiency on the one hand and the children's ability to learn any language on the other. Additional evaluation instruments are needed for this complex situation.

Overall, these data show that Language Sample Analysis can play a productive role in distinguishing language disorder from language difference and perhaps avoid some of the cultural bias of standardized language tests.

References

Loban, W. *Language Development: Kindergarten through Grade Twelve. Research Report No. 18.* Urbana, IL: National Council of Teachers of English, 1976.

Miller, J.F. *Salt Reference Database Project.* Madison, WI: University of Wisconsin-Madison, Language Analysis Laboratory, Waisman Center on Mental Retardation and Human Development, 1992.

Miller, J.F., K. Bertolino, M. Freeman, C. Freiberg, J. Larson, and J. Molaska. *Language Sample Analysis: Hmong Database Project.* Tomahawk, WI: Cooperative Educational Service Agency 9, 1990.

Wisconsin Department of Public Instruction. *Language Sample Analysis: The Wisconsin Guide.* Madison, WI: Wisconsin Department of Public Instruction, 1992.

5

Narrative Discourse Analysis

Introduction

Narrative discourse analysis focuses on the meaning the storyteller is able to construct across sentence boundaries rather than on the grammatical correctness of each sentence (Hedberg and Stoel-Gammon, 1986). Story grammar structure is seen as a cognitive scheme or representation, and therefore can be used to measure the narrator's internal organization of information (Stein and Glenn, 1979).

The initial step in narrative discourse analysis is the elicitation of the story. In the following procedures, stories are elicited under two conditions, and both narratives are analyzed in terms of story grammar structure.

Prior to analyzing a narrative, the story is transcribed and information presented in the story is organized into propositions. These propositions are units that convey important meaning distinctions. The analysis begins with a classification of propositions into informational categories. This categorization assumes that each proposition serves a function within the narrative and that any proposition can be classified only in terms of its relation to other propositions. Thus, the informational categories reflect and describe functions of propositions within narratives.

Once each proposition is classified, relations between propositions are noted. This procedure captures the temporal and causal links between events in the story. Based on the presence of informational categories and the relationships between propositions, the entire narrative is then classified in terms of story structure level. This classification is derived from patterns of proposition types and relationships noted in the story.

Story Elicitation Procedure

Narratives are elicited under two story-telling conditions, and both narratives are audiotaped for later transcription and analysis. The two story-telling conditions differ in the amount of external structure and support provided for story construction.

In the first condition, the child tells a story depicted in a wordless picture book, using the pictures as a guide. This condition, designated as "tell," provides some external structure and support for narrative construction. Although the child is allowed to use the pictures to guide the story-telling, the stories constructed are essentially self-generated.

In the second condition, the child retells the wordless picture book story without the pictures. This condition, designated "retell," provides minimal external structure and support for narrative construction because the child does not have the pictures available to guide story-telling. Although the original tellings of the story serve as a basis, the "retell" condition essentially requires autonomous use of cognitive schemes for organizing, recalling, and using narrative information.

For both story-telling conditions, the wordless picture book, *Frog on His Own* (Mayer, 1973) is used. This book depicts five sequential adventures of a frog visiting a park. In story grammar terms, each adventure represents an episode, and the five episodes are The Bee, The Picnic, The Sailboat, The Baby in the Carriage, and The Cat. Children are expected to include all five episodes in both the telling and the retelling of the story of the frog.

The procedures for eliciting stories under the tell and retell conditions are as follows.

1. Present the book to the child and say, "I have a book here that tells a story, but there are no words, just pictures. Look through the book to see what the story is. Look at the story carefully and tell me when you are done. When you are finished, I will ask you to tell me your story from this book.

2. When the child indicates he or she is finished looking through the book, place the book in front of the child, open it to the first picture, and say, "Tell me your story from this book." This step represents the tell condition. Under this condition, probes and/or questions are not permitted either during or after the telling of the story.
3. When the child has finished telling the story with the pictures, take the book away and say, "Sometimes we tell stories without books. Now, tell me your story again without using the book." This step represents the retell condition. Under this condition, probes are allowed only to prompt the child for an episode left out; questions are not permitted. When the child is finished retelling the story, and if an episode has been omitted, say, "Do you remember the part about the (bee, picnic, sailboat, baby in the carriage, cat)? Tell me that part."

Throughout the elicitation of the stories, the examiner should not make comments or ask questions while the child is narrating. The examiner may smile and nod during the child's narrative as encouragement to continue the story. In general, no cues should be provided to the child about actions or events in the story because such cues may influence the child's story grammar construction. When the child is finished, the examiner may compliment the child's effort, but other evaluative comments about the story are not permitted.

Transcription

Audiotaped stories are transcribed verbatim, including vocalized pauses, repeated words, repeated phrases, and so forth. These kinds of utterances are considered to be mazes (Loban, 1976). Although they are not included in the analysis of the narrative, mazes should be transcribed and included in brackets. The following statements represent examples of mazes.

[He jumped as far as h] he jumped as far as he can.
He thought he could ride on [um] the sailboat.
And [the cat no] the frog wanted it.
And then [they went home] they went home.

Transcribed utterances should be divided into propositions. These are informational units that roughly correspond to simple sentences. For example, the utterance "The boat sank and the little boy was crying" contains two propositions divided by a slash.

After identifying propositions, the entire narrative should be divided into sections: introduction, conclusion, and each of the five episodes of *Frog on His Own*. Only propositions included in the five episodes are subjected to further analysis.

Classification of Propositions

After the transcript is segmented into propositions, each proposition is classified as one of nine story grammar proposition types (Jax, 1989). Classification of any single proposition depends upon its relation to other propositions in the story. Thus, the classification categories reflect and describe functions of propositions within narratives, and a transcript should be read through in its entirety prior to classifying proposition types. The nine proposition types are described in Figure 14.

It is important to note that the proposition types do not necessarily need to occur in the narrative in the same order that they are listed in Figure 14. For example, a child could begin an episode with an Internal Response: "The frog was hungry." The story could then go on to describe what the frog did to solve his hunger problem.

■ **Figure 14**

Story Grammar Proposition Types

(Adapted from "Narrative Construction by Children Learning English as a Second Language: A Precursor to Reading Comprehension." Diss. University of California-Los Angeles, 1989. *Dissertation Abstracts International*, 49, 2133-A.)

• **Setting Statements** introduce the character(s), their habitual state(s), and/or location(s) as well as their changes in state or location. **Example:** "Then the frog looked at flowers."

• **Initiating Event Statements** reflect natural occurrences, actions or environmental states that trigger and/or set the stage for future planned behavior. **Example:** "And then he saw something buzzing in the flowers."

• **Action Statements** are initiating-event-type propositions that occur in the absence of future planned behavior. **Example:** "So she pulled her hand out."

• **Internal Response Statements** reflect the main character's internal state that motivates future planned behavior. **Example:** "And he wanted to know what was inside the picnic basket."

• **Plan Statements** reflect a description of the main character's strategy for attaining the goal. **Example:** "He decided to jump into the carriage to get the bottle."

• **Attempt Statements** reflect action initiated to achieve the main character's goal. **Example:** "The frog jumped to get away from the cat."

• **Consequence Statements** reflect the state that exists once all attempts to attain the goal have been completed. **Example:** "It stung the frog."

• **Reaction Statements** reflect the main character's internal feelings or thoughts about attainment or failure to attain the goal as well as the feelings or thoughts of other characters to actions in the story. **Example:** "The frog got scared."

• **Judgment Statements** reflect the narrator's evaluative or informational comments on narrated events. **Example:** "I don't think that frog is nice."

Assigning Story Grammar Structure Levels

Once each proposition is classified, each episode is assigned to one of seven story grammar structure levels (Jax, 1989). This assignment is based on patterns of story grammar proposition types as well as causal relationships noted in the narrative. The seven story grammar structure levels are described in Figure 15.

Deriving Story Grammar Structure Scores

Each episode within each narrative is assigned a story grammar structure score, with the number of points given equaling the level (for example, Level 4 = 4 points). The story reflected in the pictures of *Frog on His Own* contains five distinct episodes, and the total story grammar structure score is the sum of the scores for each episode. The potential minimum score is five (one point for each episode) and the potential maximum score is 35 (seven points for each episode) for both the tell and the retell conditions.

Appendix Q includes an annotated example of a coded transcript.

True normative data are not available for development of narrative abilities in school-age children. However, some preliminary data are available on small samples of Hmong children, and these date can be used to interpret narrative construction abilities in these children in a descriptive fashion.

Story Grammar Structure Levels

(Adapted from "Narrative Construction by Children Learning English as a Second Language: A Precursor to Reading Comprehension." Diss. University of California-Los Angeles, 1989. *Dissertation Abstracts International,* 49, 2133-A.)

Level I: Descriptive Sequences describe character(s), setting, and habitual activity without indicating causal relationships.

Level II: Action Sequences describe a chronological list of actions without indicating causal relationships.

Level III: Reactive Sequences describe circumstances that automatically cause change in a state of affairs without planning or intentionality.

Level IV: Abbreviated Episodes imply the goals of the main character, but do not indicate purposeful planning or action. Propositions include an Initiating Event + a Consequence OR an Internal Response + a Consequence.

Level V: Complete Episodes provide evidence of planning in the description of purposeful activity. Propositions include Setting, Consequence, and at least two of the following types: Initiating Event, Internal Response, Attempt.

Level VI: Complex Episodes elaborate Complete Episodes by developing multiple attempt-consequence sequences and/or by embedding lower level story structures into the episode structure.

Level VII: Interactive Episodes describe the goals, attempts, and consequences of at least two characters who influence each other, providing Complete Episodes from each character's perspective.

The Sample

These data represent story grammar construction performances of 44 typically developing Hmong children in the second, fourth, and fifth grades in public schools in Wisconsin. The entire data set represents a composite of results from two studies.

One study was conducted for the Department of Public Instruction (DPI) as part of a project on assessment of linguistically and culturally diverse children. For that study, second- and fifth-grade children were randomly sampled from schools in four communities across the state (Eau Claire, La Crosse, Sheboygan, Wausau). There were 14 children in the second grade sample and 19 children in the fifth-grade sample.

The second study was conducted in the Eau Claire schools and was designed to explore language skills in Hmong and language-learning disabled children in the fourth grade. For that study, children were nominated by teachers on the grounds of language background and academic achievement levels. Eleven children were included in the study.

In the combined sample of 44 children, there were more boys than girls, but gender distribution was equivalent across grade groupings and significant differences in story grammar structure were not noted between groups defined by gender. All of the children had received ESL services prior to data collection, and some were still receiving ESL instruction at the time of data collection.

Forty-three (98 percent) of the children were judged as fluent in English, and all of the children were placed in English-only mainstream classrooms for their primary instruction. All of the children were considered to be functioning adequately in those classrooms, and they demonstrated reading comprehension skills that ranged form below average to above average for their grades. None of the children demonstrated any overt physical, sensory, or cognitive deficits, and none had been referred for special education consideration.

These characteristics of the children from whom the narrative samples were drawn suggest that the results can be considered representative of typically achieving Hmong children in the state.

Relationships in the Data

Figure 16 reflects story grammar structure scores for each grade level under the two story-telling conditions. The scores reflect complexity of stories, with higher scores indicating greater complexity of story grammar structure use. While the scores are not inherently meaningful for clinical application, patterns noted in the scores suggest grounds for clinical interpretation.

As reflected in Figure 16, use of story grammar structure complexity increases with age. Although significant differences in story complexity were noted only between the second and the fifth graders, story complexity increased progressively across the grades, suggesting developmental sensitivity of this narrative analysis measure.

■ **Figure 16**

Story Grammar Structure Scores by Condition and Grade Level

Condition	2nd grade (n=14)	4th grade (n=11)	5th grade (n=19)
Tell*	11.79	13.09	14.63
Retell**	11.43	13.73	15.37

*F = 5.71; p<.01; second<fifth, p= .05
**F = 9.16; p<.01; second<fifth, p=.05

Figure 17 reflects differences in story grammar complexity for the three groups in an alternative form. These data show the story grammar structure levels used by each group of children, and the values reported reflect the percentage of occurrence of each structure level across episodes under both the tell and the retell conditions.

All groups tended to use proportionately more Action Sequence (Level II) and Reactive Sequence (Level III) structures than other higher level structures. However, Action Sequences were the primary story grammar structure used by the second graders, whereas the fifth graders' stories were distributed more evenly across Levels II and III. The fourth graders' performances fell between these extremes.

For all grades, story grammar structure complexity shifted from the tell to the retell condition. However, within each grade level, different patterns emerged in this shift. These patterns are reflected in the data in Figures 16 and 17.

■ **Figure 17**

Story Grammar Structure Levels by Condition and Grade Level

	Tell			Retell		
Grade	2nd	4th	5th	2nd	4th	5th
Total No. Episodes	70	55	95	70	55	94
Level I	---	---	---	---	1.8%	---
Level II	77.1%	65.5%	50.5%	78.6%	52.7%	39.4%
Level III	14.3%	18.2%	26.3%	17.1%	27.3%	33.0%
Level IV	4.3%	7.3%	6.3%	1.4%	9.1%	9.6%
Level V	4.3%	7.3%	14.7%	2.9%	7.3%	14.9%
Level VI	---	1.8%	1.1%	---	1.8%	2.1%
Level VII	---	---	1.1%	---	---	1.1%

% Retell Prompts				1.6%	.6%	.1%

Level I = Descriptive Sequence; Level II = Action Sequence; Level III = Reactive Sequence; Level IV = Abbreviated Episode; Level V = Complete Episode; Level VI = Complex Episode; Level VII = Interactive Episode.
T = 1.76, P = .05; second graders > fifth graders

The data in Figure 17 indicate that the second graders showed an increase in proportion of Level II and III structures and a decrease in higher level structures from tell to retell. In contrast, the fourth and fifth graders showed a decrease in proportion of Level II structures and an increase in higher level structures from tell to retell.

The data in Figure 17 highlight that, for the second graders, stories became less complex, whereas for the fourth and fifth graders stories became more complex from tell to retell. Although not significant, this trend may become more pronounced in a larger sample. However, the shift under the retell condition to more complex usage by the fourth and fifth graders, and the concomitant shift to less complex usage by the second graders, suggests that the older children were more effective in using story grammar structure as an internal heuristic for organizing information for later retrieval and use.

This conclusion is supported by differences across the grade levels in the number of prompts needed for complete story-telling under the retell condition. The second graders required more prompting than children in the other grades to recall the story they had told under the tell condition, although the difference was significant only between the second and fifth graders. This finding suggests that the second graders were less able than the older children to use story grammar structure as an organizational scheme.

Higher story grammar scores were associated with higher reading comprehension levels.

Taken together, results of these analyses suggest that measures of grammatical structure complexity and discourse structure complexity are moderately related to each other. Although both types of measures of oral language proficiency can distinguish Hmong children at different age levels, grammatical measures do not predict reading achievement whereas discourse measures contribute to such prediction. This finding suggests the need to include evaluation of both aspects of oral language in assessments of language proficiency of Hmong children.

Use of Data

Interpretations of developmental adequacy of narrative discourse should consider evidence of complexity of story grammar structure as well as evidence of use of story grammar structure as an organizational scheme. Story structure complexity is seen in the telling of stories that reflect higher levels of story grammar structure. Use of story grammar structure as an organizational scheme is seen in increases in story complexity from tell to retell conditions as well as in the relative amount of prompting needed for story completion under the retell condition.

Accordingly, these data can be used descriptively in diagnostic decision making, and the following guidelines are suggested.

For second graders, narrative skills of Hmong children can be considered to be within normal limits if stories reflect primarily Level II (Action Sequence) and Level III (Reactive Sequence) structures, if story complexity decreases from tell to retell, and if relatively extensive prompting is required under the retell condition.

For fourth graders, narrative skills of Hmong children can be considered to be within normal limits if stories reflect primarily Level II (Action Sequence) and Level III (Reactive Sequence) structures but also include some higher level story grammar structures, if story complexity increases from tell to retell, and if some prompting is necessary under the retell condition.

For fifth graders, narrative skills of Hmong children can be considered to be within normal limits if stories contain a full range of components reflecting both lower and higher level story grammar structures, if story complexity increases from tell to retell, and if occasional prompting is necessary under the retell condition.

References

Canale, M. "On Some Theoretical Frameworks for Language Proficiency." In *Language Proficiency and Academic Achievement*. Ed. C. Rivera. Clevedon, England: Multilingual Matters, Ltd., 1984, pp. 28-40.

Carpenter, L.J. "Including Multicultural Content in the Undergraduate Communication Disorders Curriculum." Unpublished manuscript, University of Wisconsin-Eau Claire, 1990.

Carpenter, L.J. "The Influence of Examiner Knowledge Base on Diagnostic Decision Making with Language Minority Children." *The Journal of Educational Issues of Language Minority Students* 11 (1992), pp. 139-161.

Carpenter, L.J. "Narrative Construction in Hmong and LLD Children." Paper presented at the annual convention of the Wisconsin Speech Language Hearing Association, Oshkosh, May 1992.

Damico, J.S. "Descriptive Assessment of Communicative Ability in Limited-English Proficient Students." In *Limiting Bias in the Assessment of Bilingual Students*. Eds. E.V. Hamayan and J.S. Damico. Austin, TX: Pro-ed, 1991, pp. 158-217.

Duran, R., et al. "TOEFL from a Communicative Viewpoint on Language Proficiency: A Working Paper" (Report No. ETS-RR-85-8). Princeton, NJ: Educational Testing Service, 1985.

Hedberg, N.L., and C. Stoel-Gammon. "Narrative Analysis: Clinical Procedures." *Topics in Language Disorders* 7.1 (1986), pp. 58-68.

Jax, V.A. "Narrative Construction by Children Learning English as a Second Language: A Precursor to Reading Comprehension." Diss. University of California-Los Angeles, 1989. Dissertation Abstracts International, 49, 2133-A.

Loban, W. *Language Development: Kindergarten Through Grade Twelve*. Urbana, IL: National Council of Teachers of English, 1976.

Mayer, M. *Frog on His Own*. New York, NY: Dial Books for Young Readers, 1973.

Ortiz, A.A., and S.B. Garcia. "A Pre-referral Process for Preventing Inappropriate Referrals of Hispanic Students to Special Education." In *Schools and the Culturally Diverse Exceptional Student: Promising Practices and Future Directions*. Eds. A.A. Ortiz and B.A. Ramirez. Reston, VA: The Council for Exceptional Children, 1988, pp. 6-18.

Roth, F.P., and N.J. Spekman. "Narrative Discourse: Spontaneously Generated Stories of Learning Disabled and Normally Achieving Students." *Journal of Speech and Hearing Disorders,* 51 (1986), pp. 8-23.

Rueda, R., et al. *Final Report- Longitudinal Study I Report: An Examination of Special Education Decision Making with Hispanic First Time Referrals in Large Urban School Districts*. Los Alamitos, CA: Handicapped-Minority Research Institute, 1985.

Stein, N., and C. Glenn. "An Analysis of Story Comprehension in Elementary School Children." In *New Directions in Discourse Processing*. vol. 2. Ed. R.O. Freedle. Norwood, NJ: Ablex Publishing Corporation, 1979, pp. 53-120.

Ulibarri, D.M., M.L. Spencer, and G.A. Rivas. "Language Proficiency and Academic Achievement: A Study of Language Proficiency Tests and their Relationship to School Ratings as Predictors of Academic Achievement." *NABE* Journal 5 (1981), pp. 47-80.

U.S. Congress. P.L. 94-142, 20 USC 1401 et. seq.

Westby, C.E. "Learning to Talk, Talking to Learn: Oral-Literate Language Differences." In *Communication Skills and Classroom Success: Therapy Methodologies for Language-Learning Disabled Students*. Ed. C.S. Simon. San Diego, CA: College Hill Press, 1985, pp. 181-213.

6

Intervention

Introduction

This chapter provides regular education classroom teachers with perspectives on working with children from linguistically and culturally diverse (LCD) backgrounds who do not have exceptional educational needs (EEN).

The American Speech-Language-Hearing Association (ASHA), in its position paper on social dialects, states that a language difference should not be equated with a language disorder. "It is the role of the classroom teacher, NOT the speech (and) language pathologist, to teach standard English and/or English as a second language (ESL). Bilingual teachers, ESL teachers, and speech (and) language pathologists may serve as consultants to the classroom teacher, but the major responsibility for teaching standard English lies with the classroom teacher."

Teachers should consider the following perspectives when teaching students who have limited-English proficiency (LEP) or who use non-standard English dialects.

- All varieties of English are linguistically valid and have communicative and cultural value.
- The teaching of standard English to non-standard or new speakers of English does not mean, and must not mean, eradication of the non-standard dialect or native language of the speaker.
- Educators must accept language and speech differences (such as dialects) in informal conversation. The teacher must focus on what the student says (meaning), not how he or she says it (grammar and speech production). The teacher should model correct patterns of standard English and should correct errors positively rather than negatively so the student does not become discouraged from further attempts at using standard English.
- Natural conversational experiences are the best tools for acquiring and practicing a new language or dialect. Teachers should take advantage of natural opportunities that abound throughout the school environment and academic curriculum to provide such experiences. Examples include art projects, field trips, role playing, filmstrips, videos and videotaping, science projects and experiments, journal writing, and cocurricular and extracurricular activities.
- Educators must be sensitive to each student's cultural background and must validate the importance of the cultures' values and attitudes. Teachers should consider the culture's customs and attitudes toward education, the family's socioeconomic status, how cultural values are maintained in the home, the student's level of proficiency in standard English, and, when appropriate, the student's and parents' chosen language/dialect. Teachers should bring multiculturalism into classrooms by using multicultural calendars, personal life histories, folk tales, and guest speakers from diverse cultures.
- Dialect and second language instruction is most effective when explicit linguistic and communicative features of the student's first language or dialect are compared with those of standard English.
- Educators should combine auditory, visual, and kinesthetic cues to introduce new or unfamiliar linguistic, academic, or cultural concepts.
- Cooperative learning and peer support groups provide opportunities for sharing feelings and experiences with teachers and peers.
- Understanding precedes production.

Strategies for African American Students

In *Sensitizing Teachers to Cultural Differences: An African American Perspective*, Evelyn Baker Dandy states that "black communication is not just a speech code, it is a system of communication."

Teachers must find ways to become aware of linguistic and cultural differences, trying new approaches and adapting curriculum to methods that nurture the student's potential without devaluing the student or his or her language. Teachers also must become familiar with the linguistic and cultural diversity of their students and with word meanings that often are changed to confuse listeners who are not part of the group.

Dandy also suggests that teachers use commonly practiced verbal strategies to move students from African American English to standard English without destroying the students' self-concept. Rappin' is one verbal strategy African Americans frequently use. Rappin' is a colorful or distinctive style of talking into which speakers inject their own personality to provide information, convince or persuade, introduce themselves, and communicate through music.

Rap puts the speaker in a position of control. African Americans take pride in their communicative style. If through their rappin' they can absorb their audience in conversation, the speaker is successful. Dandy (1990, quoting Smitherman, 1977) uses Richard Wright's *Black Boy* to illustrate a typical street corner rap in which she describes each line in parentheses.

- "You eat yet?" (uneasily, trying to make conversation)
- "Yeah, man, I done really fed my face." (casually)
- "I had cabbage and potatoes." (confidently)
- "I had buttermilk and black-eyed peas." (merely informational)

The same kind of rap is often heard in schools and can be transformed into learning situations

In *Treatment of Communication Disorders in Culturally and Linguistically Diverse Populations*, Orlando Taylor suggests that teachers use A Cultural and Communicative Program for Teaching (ACCPT), a child-centered approach to intervention. The focus of this approach is on teaching standard English as a second dialect. Taylor advocates an eight-step approach to teaching oral communication.

Step 1: Positive attitude toward one's own language. It is a model based on the belief that a student's home or community dialect can be preserved as he or she learns standard English. Respect for one's own language is prerequisite to learning a second dialect as well as for the languages of others.

Step 2: Awareness of language varieties. Ample opportunity for dialect speakers to experience linguistic varieties is provided. For example, this can be done by reading a story in standard English, then in the child's dialect or language and in the languages of all of the other non-standard English speakers in the room. At this stage, specific licenses and differences are not emphasized.

Step 3: Recognizing, labeling, and contrasting dialects. In order for a student to be able to take advantage of step 3, he or she must be able to step outside of himself or herself to analyze the elements of what they are hearing. However, it is unnecessary for a child to be able to label a feature in order to be able to reproduce it.

Step 4: Comprehension of meaning. In this developmental sequence, comprehension is narrowly defined as the underlying meaning of the dialectical term being used. "I need a tonic" usually means medicinal stimulant in California, but in New English is generally means a soda.

Step 5: Recognition of situational requirements. Lessons are designed so students learn to focus on function. Students are taught how to asses what is appropriate and what is inappropriate in specific communication situations.

Step 6: Production in structured situations. Students are taught the production of certain language forms at this level. The student is given an opportunity to practice standard English in certain situations, with help from the teacher (e.g., a script, a written passage [prose or poetry] etc.). Choral reading is an effective technique.

Step 7: Production in controlled situations involves lessons in which the student learns to produce targeted features of the new dialect without external assistance. Role playing and storytelling are good examples of activities. A key factor is that the situation is controlled by the teacher and the student, in that the communication situation, the audience, and the intention are defined in advance.

Step 8: Production in spontaneous situations. This is the final phase of the developmental program. Lessons are designed to allow the student to determine the linguistic and communicative requirements of the situation, audience, or topic and then proceed the actual forms in real-life experience in that circumstance.

African American scholars describe the African-centered view as applied to education as Afrocentricity (Dandy, 1990, p. 110). All teachers have an obligation to become informed about the contributions of African Americans and the African cultural influence. Culturally sensitive teachers

• seek to understand culturally acceptable modes of communication other than their own.
• recognize that Black English is derived from the collision of the many languages of Africa and European English. The collision resulted in a distinct linguistic form in much the same way as the development of American English; it simply evolved in somewhat different ways and for different reasons.
• set goals to build communicative competence in the standard dialect without degrading the dialect of the students.
• teach students to distinguish between dialect renderings and standard English by
   —providing ample opportunities for students to communicate in speaking and writing
   —setting up role-play situations wherein students have to select the most appropriate language for the situation or audience (for example, formal or informal language, school talk, home talk, or street talk).
   —allowing students time to learn from one another by using whole language, cooperative learning, writing to read, and invented spelling.
   —teaching about the contributions African Americans have made to science, math, language arts, history, and other content areas.
   —searching for connections between language systems by studying the culture and language and by infusing the concept of Afrocentricity into the schools.
• work with librarians to provide books about African Americans (for example, J.E. Hale-Benson's *Black Children: Their Roots, Culture and Learning Styles* and E.B. Dandy's *Black Child*).

Strategies for Hmong and other Students

Educators must be sensitive to each student's cultural background and must validate the importance of the cultures' values and attitudes. Teachers should consider the culture's customs and attitudes toward education, the family's socioeconomic status, how cultural values are maintained in the home, the student's level of proficiency in standard English, and when appropriate, the student's and parents' chosen home language. Teachers should bring multiculturalism into classrooms by using multicultural calendars, personal life histories, folk tales, and guest speakers from diverse cultures. More specific suggestions include

● Ask the students about their backgrounds and experiences and enthusiastically assign their history as a social studies project; engage the entire school in international education. The more teachers and other students learn from students from linguistically and culturally diverse backgrounds, the sooner the student will feel confident and comfortable.

● Go to the library, read National Geographic; invite multicultural speakers to the school; keep current on movies, traveling exhibits, and local festivals; and listen to and read the news and discuss pertinent issues with the class.

● Find out which holidays the students celebrate and how they are celebrated. Find out whether their customs are similar to American customs. Have the students make flags and foods from different countries. Students may have clothes, money, photos, artwork, songs, games, maps, and alphabet or number charts to share. All are valid educational media. Invite parents to teach their native languages. Celebrate "Holidays Around the World."

Whenever time permits, teachers should explain, demonstrate, and anticipate possible difficulties with everyday routines and regulations. School district policies for parents and students should be translated into their native language. Depending upon the student's experiences with formal education, the need for explanations may vary greatly. The following classroom routines can be used as teaching opportunities to prepare the students for school.

● rules (rewards, enforcement, consequences)
● conduct
● morning rituals (greetings, calendar work, assignments, collection of money and homework)
● library conduct (checkout, book return)
● field trips and permission slips
● gym (participation, showers, attire)
● substitute teachers
● tests, quizzes, reports
● grades, report cards, incomplete
● snacks
● free time
● teams (choosing, assigning)
● standardized testing (exemptions)
● special projects (extra credit, double grades)

Information about the following general school routines also help prepare students for school.
● breaks: bathroom, water, recess
● cafeteria rules: line formation, lunch passes
● fire drills, tornado drills
● assemblies, pep rallies, awards, award ceremonies
● contests, competition
● fund raisers
● routine health exams, screening
● suspension
● guidance counseling

- disciplinary methods (in-school suspension)
- free lunch (income verification)
- family and consumer education

Afterschool activities (such as parent conferences, parent-teacher organization meetings, dances and other special events, athletics, and summer school) also help students and their families learn about school.

Teachers should structure classroom interaction so that all students can participate and feel successful in their contribution. They should

- speak simply and clearly to all students; try to speak in short, complete sentences in a normal tone of voice. It is not necessary to speak loudly.
- use prompts, cues, facial expressions, body language, visual aids, and concrete objects as often as possible. Pointing and nodding toward an open door while saying, "Please shut the door" is much more effective than giving the command in an isolated context.
- keep communication lines open. If the student is in an English as a Second Language class, let the teacher know what goes on in your class. The consistency and repetition of concepts and/or lessons can help the student.
- call on all students as much as possible. For example, if a student cannot speak much English, have him or her come to the board to point to the map, complete the number line, circle the answer, and so forth.
- provide sufficient time for students from linguistically and culturally diverse backgrounds to complete the transition from one language and/or culture to another. Allow children to speak their native language until they feel comfortable speaking the language of the mainstream culture.
- allow the students to use their language/dialect during social situations, for example at recess and for more technical and/or emergency situations.
- keep talking to the student. It is normal for the student to experience a "silent period" that can last days, weeks, or even months. In order to learn the language, the student must first develop active listening skills, followed by speaking, reading, and writing.

It is important for the teacher to evaluate the student's understanding in academic areas. For example

—use a variety of testing tools.
—adjust tests to student's ability.
—give student opportunity to demonstrate knowledge in ways that do not require language.
—use oral instead of written tests.
—have a test read to the student.
—be specific in asking questions.
—give student sufficient time to complete the test.
—divide tested material into manageable sections.
—use peers to check work.

Each teacher is responsible for individualizing, adapting, and modifying classwork for the student, while taking into consideration the student's language development, study skills, and the subject content.

The following commonly asked questions or common concerns of ESL teachers are adapted from the Wausau School District's *ESL Handbook for Classroom Teachers* by Lynell Anderson.

1. Is the teacher feeling pressured by demands of material that must be taught to students?
    - It is not expected that all students have similar background experiences. Their learning is a gradual process.
    - Remember that it is impossible to provide all necessary background.
    - Modify content by deciding what is most important and appropriate for the students to learn.
    - Modify expectations of students according to language ability.

- Adapt materials if necessary.
- Use the buddy system.

2. What if the student speaks in his or her native language or dialect during class?
   - The use of native language or dialect is necessary in certain situations (for example, clarifying content when working with a buddy, vocabulary explanation, directions).
   - Work with the students to establish classroom rules for appropriate use of native language or dialect.
   —Encourage whispering during interpretation of materials.
   —Develop a sign or signal to monitor noise level.
   —Allow for this important interaction.
   —Encourage participation in English. Do join the conversation in English. Don't use negative comments such as "Don't speak Hmong". or "Don't use your dialect."
   - Communicate rules to all students.

3. What if the student doesn't understand a concept in a particular content area?
   - Use a wide assortment of visuals.
   - Use hands-on activities that involve the student in learning.
   - Use the buddy system to explain the concept.
   - Arrange tutoring for the child.

4. What if students don't integrate with mainstream students?
   - Arrange integrated seating within the classroom.
   - Assign integrated grouping.
   - Encourage students to participate in extracurricular activities, but be aware that not all parents understand the value of these activities. (Most parents want the best academic education for their children.)
   - Be aware of the student's comfort level. Some students need time to converse freely in their own language. These times can be recess, lunch, or before and after school.
   - Understand that students will more naturally integrate as their English confidence improves.
   - Recognize that fear of the unfamiliar exists for all students.

5. What if students have difficulty with written work?
   - Remember that writing is a higher level, developmental skill.
   - Provide regular opportunities for writing practice.
   - Provide varied pre-writing experiences, semantic mapping, story framing, and so forth.
   - Consider grading for content rather than mechanics. Use holistic grading of written material.

6. What if students are hesitant to speak in class?
   - Understand the student's fear of making mistakes in front of classmates.
   - Remember that in some cultures, students are afraid of being disrespectful to authority figures. Students respect teachers as authority figures in the classroom and may find it difficult to ask questions or make eye contact.
   - Use non-threatening body language when communicating to students.
   - Be aware that students worry about not being understood because of pronunciation.
   - Encourage students to keep trying while remaining sensitive to the individual's readiness levels.

7. What if students return from ESL or other programs while a lesson is in progress?
   - Integrate the students into the lesson.
   - Have a buddy help integrate them into the lesson in progress.
   - Establish clear guidelines for independent work.
   - Have materials available for student choice such as listening to tapes, working on flashcards, writing a journal, practicing cursive, or working on computers.

References

American Speech-Language-Hearing Association. "Position Paper on Social Dialects." *ASHA*, September 1983.

Anderson, Lynell. *ESL Handbook for Classroom Teachers*. Wausau, WI: Wausau School District, 1993.

Damico, Jack S., and Else V. Hamayan *Multicultural Language Intervention: Addressing Cultural and Linguistic Diversity*. Buffalo, NY: Educom Associates, 1992, pp. 66-67.

Dandy, Evelyn Baker. "Sensitizing Teachers to Cultural Differences: An African American Perspective." Paper presented at the National Dropout Prevention Conference, Nashville, TN. March 25-27, 1990.

Gruenewald, Lee J., and Sara A. Pollak. *Language Interaction in Curriculum and Instruction*. Austin, TX: Pro-ed, 1990.

Garcia, Shernaz B., and Diana H. Malking. "Toward Defining Programs and Services for Culturally and Linguistically Diverse Learners in Special Education." *Teaching Exceptional Children*, Fall 1993, pp. 52-58.

La Crosse School District. *ESL Handbook for Classroom Teachers*. La Crosse, WI: La Crosse School District.

Lee, Felicia R. "Grappling with How to Teach Young Speakers of Black Dialect." *New York Times* 5 Jan. 1994.

National Clearinghouse on Bilingual Education

Savignon, S. *Communicative Competence: Theory and Classroom Practice*. Boston: Addison-Wesley, 1983.

Seelye, H.N. *Teaching Culture: Strategies for Intercultural Communication*. Lincolnwood, IL: National Textbook Company, 1984.

Smitherman, G. *Talkin' and Testifyin': The Language of Black America*. Detroit, MI: Wayne State University Press, 1986 (original work published 1977, Boston: Houghton Mifflin).

Taylor, Orlando. *Treatment of Communication Disorders in Culturally and Linguistically Diverse Populations*. San Diego, CA: College Hill Press, 1986.

7

Case Studies

African American
Hmong

African American

Name: Louis, C.A.
Age: 9 years, 9 months
Grade: 4

Reason for Referral

Louis was referred at the beginning of fourth grade because he was unable to read, did not participate in class and used language for basic needs only. He has extremely low ability in language arts. He has minimum oral language, low speech intelligibility, and difficulty relating to peers. Classroom responses are short, and he rarely shares the important events in his life. He has not developed relationships with other students. He is always on guard as any reading, writing, or speaking activity will demonstrate his inabilities.

- uses speech and language for basic needs only
- has difficulty in all academic area
- has not developed relationships with peers

Background Information

It is reported that Louis developed normally except for his speech and language skills. He began to say words by the age of 2. His mother reported that few people can understand him though she understands him. Louis' mother is quiet and talks very little. Louis' sister is in the third grade. She has no difficulty verbally interacting with peers or adults and is doing well in school. Louis attended Head Start and has been in three different schools since kindergarten. He uses African American English.

- normal development noted
- family background unavailable
- note if African American English is used
- previous interventions

Previous Interventions

Records were unavailable but Louis' mother stated that he received speech and language therapy while attending school in a different state.

Current Placement

Louis is enrolled in a regular fourth-grade classroom. He has been referred for a possible learning disability and a possible speech and language disorder by his regular classroom teacher due to difficulties in academic and verbal areas.

- present grade placement
- any exceptional educuational needs

Hearing Evaluation

A hearing screening indicated no difficulties at the present time, and no concerns were noted by the teacher or parent.

- hearing screening is mandatory (Appendix P)
- if screening indicates any concerns, a full audiological assessment should be conducted

Vision Evaluation

A vision screening indicated no difficulties at the present time, and the teacher and parent noted no concerns.

Tests Administered

Peabody Picture Vocabulary Test-Revised (Form M)
Expressive 1-Word Picture Vocabulary Test-R
Systematic Analysis of Language Transcripts Observations
- note standardized test bias—what populations are they normed on?
- take a language sample
- utilize LSA
- select a battery of tests of differential diagnosis

Test Results

Peabody Picture Vocabulary Test, SS 77, 2nd percentile
Expressive 1-Word Picture Vocabulary Test-R, SS 5, 4th percentile
Stanine 2

The inability to understand and label common objects or items negatively impacts on one's ability to understand and participate in regular classroom activities.

Systematic Analysis of Language Transcripts

SALT was chosen as the best means of evaluating expressive language. It is a standard method of collecting, recording, transcribing, and analyzing language samples. It is related to the kind of language skills needed to perform well academically. It also carries with it none of the bias that may be present in other standardized language assessment measures for children who come from linguistically and culturally diverse communities. Sensitive and cautious use of data is necessary when children come from other than the mainstream culture.

The narrative language sample was analyzed using SALT and compared to the typically developing 9-year-olds in the reference database (*LSA, The Wisconsin Guide*, 1992). Because the narrative sample was more easily understood than the conversation sample, it was chosen for analysis.

Measurement Category	Student	Standard Deviation	9-year-old Database
MLU	5.08	1.64	8.80
No. complete words	386	104	473
Words/minute	52.76	21.29	125.94
No. of pauses	202.62		
Pause time between utterances	1.77 minutes	-4 s.d.	10 seconds
Mazes	9	15	31

A general summary of the narrative language sample data found that a greater amount of time was needed to produce fewer utterances that are far shorter and less complex than typically developing 9-year-olds. It was also found that Louis produced significantly fewer utterances containing mazes and fewer maze words. His utterances were so short that they hardly afford the opportunity to be disorganized. In the area of word listed, Louis produced fewer total conjunctions and fewer types of conjunctions. This data reflects the lack of complexity in Louis' utterances. His use of the bound morphemes /ing, /s and z are below the mean expected.

African American English

Louis uses African American English. These forms are not marked as errors in a SALT transcript. They are marked as an indication of the child's use of the ethnic dialect. Louis' use of African American English does not make comprehension of his language more difficult. It is not the source of his speech and language difficulties. Examples of the African American English forms that Louis uses are as follows

"When Gina killed Martin mother bird."

Martin(s) and mother(s) are examples of non-obligatory possessive markers. Note that Louis used the past tense in the word "killed" in the above example, but he did not in the following example.

"They didn't show when it happen."

It is typical for African American children to mix standard and African American English in both oral and written language; sometimes using standard forms, other times using African American English forms.

"This man, he a policeman , <and> they kill him."

This is an example of pronoun repetition of the subject for emphasis or a pronominal apposition because a pronoun is used to restate the subject.

"He eat that stuff"

is an example of non-obligatory third person marker with the word "eat(s)."

"This all I can remember"

is an example of an auxiliary deletion of the word "is."

Observations

In the classroom, Louis responded to direct questions but always with a very short response. He doesn't share important events in his life, like the birth of his baby brother. He could not follow oral directions given to his class by the teacher. She must always go to him separately and break each direction into smaller, specific parts. If he faces an obstacle in understanding his classwork, he may act out inappropriately. His teacher feels that his frustration with his limitations in reading, writing, and speaking leads to the behavior that gets him into difficulty.

Louis does not discuss spontaneously even in small groups. He never shares information and thus never develops relationships with other students.
- observe student in various settings (for example, classroom, lunch room, playground)
- observe peer interaction, classroom teacher/child, volunteering, nonverbal communication

Summary

The Language Sample Analysis, classroom observation, and standardized test results confirmed Louis' low production of speech and language. Louis has a speech and language disorder that significantly interferes with his educational success and interpersonal relationships. His utterances are far shorter and less complex than typically developing 9-year-olds.

In order to promote and reinforce verbal participation within the regular classroom, Louis needs the vocabulary and topics in advance so he can begin to feel success.

Hmong

Name: Chue, C.A.
Age: 7 years, 6 months
Grade: 2

Reason for referral

Chue was referred by his second-grade teacher, who was concerned about his poor academic achievement and his poor verbal language skills. He does not verbally (English) participate in the classroom. As reported by the Hmong interpreter, Chue's verbal skills in Hmong, both content and complexity, are noted as being poor compared with other Hmong children his age. Initially, he was thought to be shy, giving a smile and a blank stare when he was questioned in class. His parents report that he is slow to respond to questions at home, where Hmong is spoken. Results of an initial academic screening in the regular second-grade class indicated reading, math, and spelling achievement at a mid-first grade level. Performance skills appear to be higher than verbal skills when observed across different classroom settings.

- difficulties in all academic areas
- resists verbal participation even with peers
- regular and ESL teacher input
- verbal skills lower than performance
- CAUTION: do not report standardized scores

Background Information

Chue's father gave the background information through the school's Hmong interpreter. Chue was born in America and is the second youngest of six children. All the children in the family have been in the English as a Second Language program in the school district. Health history suggests trauma at the time of birth when Chue experienced difficulties with breathing. It also was reported that Chue was born with bruises around his neck, which were thought to be the result of the umbilical cord being around his neck and head. High fevers also have been reported in his early health history. Hearing difficulties have been reported and hearing acuity has been questioned.

Hmong is the language of choice in the home. Chue's father speaks Hmong and English. Chue's mother has limited English skills. Conversations in the home are primarily in Hmong although some English is spoken between the father and other siblings. Chue responds verbally to Hmong and English. Chue's father says Chue's responses in Hmong and English are "incomplete, and are hard to follow. He doesn't talk in complete thought."

- family background obtained through a Hmong interpreter
- health history obtained with help of interpreter (for example, birth trauma, breathing problems, high fevers, other medical difficulties, family health history)
- Note: language dominance vs. language preference
- processing difficulties questioned
- interpreter reported difficulty in first language
- utterance completeness questioned

Previous Interventions

Chue has been enrolled in the preschool English as a Second Language (ESL) program since he was 3 years old and in an ESL kindergarten where he was identified at Level 2 of Limited English Proficiency (LEP) (he understands simple sentences in English, but he speaks only isolated words and expressions). In kindergarten he was identified at Level 3

LEP based on his performance on the Pre-Las. When he entered the second grade, he was given a Level 4 LEP status (the student responds in coherent, fluent English appropriate for his age). His progress in the LEP levels suggests his understanding of the English language is progressing adequately.
- always report previous interventions (for example, preschool, English as a Second Language, Head Start)
- retentions or school changes
- special programs or programming

Current Placement

Chue is enrolled in a regular second grade classroom and is no longer seen by the ESL teacher. He has been referred for a possible learning disability and speech and language evaluation by his regular classroom teacher due to difficulties in the academic and verbal areas.
- Note: LEP system used in your district (see Appendix T)
- present grade placement
- ESL involvement
- any exceptional educational needs

Hearing Evaluation

A history of hearing difficulties has been reported. He failed the regular school hearing screenings, and he has had an audiological evaluation that indicates a mild conductive hearing loss at the present time. He is on medication for an infection.
- hearing screening is mandatory
- if screening indicated any concerns a full audiological assessment should be conducted

Vision Screening

A vision screening indicated no difficulties at the present time, and the teacher and parents noted no concerns.

Tests Administered

Peabody Picture Vocabulary Test-Revised (Form L)
Receptive One Word Picture Vocabulary Test
Expressive One Word Picture Vocabulary Test
Fisher Logemann Articulation Test
Test of Oral Language Development (Oral Vocabulary Subtest)
Story Tell-Retell
Language Sample Analysis (narrative and conversation
Observations
- Note: Use extreme caution when interpreting standardized test results with linguistically and culturally diverse population (see Appendix E for test bias information)
- Note: Test items that may be culturally biased
- utilize an interpreter who speaks the language of the student (for example, Hmong or Lao)
- take a language sample
- utilize Language Sample Analysis
- select a battery of tests for a differential diagnosis

Test Results

The following tests were used in a modified manner only to gain additional information. Because of the bias nature of the tests, results must be viewed with great caution. Results can only be viewed in a criterion-referenced way and not valid in terms of numerical equivalents, because these tests have not been normed on Hmong students.

The assessment was completed with the assistance of the Hmong interpreter.

On the Peabody Picture Vocabulary Test (PPVT) and the Receptive One Word Picture Vocabulary Test (ROWPVT), Chue demonstrated better understanding of single words in Hmong than in English, when asked to point to specific pictorial representations of vocabulary words. It must be noted, however, that many of the words presented in Hmong are descriptive rather than single words (for example, for the word "faucet" it is necessary to say the handle that turns the water on and off rather than just the word "faucet.") The modification of the test suggests that he was able to understand and process single-word receptive vocabulary.

On the Expressive One Word Picture Vocabulary Test, Chue identified many of the age-appropriate words. When he was unsure of a word he attempted to define or describe the word. He would often name parts of the whole (horse for merry-go-round) or would continue to describe ("like it goes like, um, you know [demonstrates with his hands] it goes up; no it goes round.") For thermometer, Chue said "that thing that you put, um, you put it in your mouth and, um, it take, it says if you hot or not."

On the Test of Oral Language Development, Chue thought about the word presented for a few moments, began a thought, would often abort the thought and would begin again. It was often difficult to follow the thoughts because of revisions and attempts to repair the information (for example: face—"the thing, everybody gots, it you know it can eat and it round and sometimes you draw it." and baby—"it little, my mom gots, my mom and dad gots a little baby, but they not little now."

On the Story Tell-Retell, Chue was asked to tell a story with the use of a wordless picture book. Chue looked through the book and appeared to study the pictures on each of the pages. During the story tell portion of the tape-recorded sample, Chue basically labeled and described the people and the situations. He was able to determine the main character and could describe the basic actions and/or events.

When asked to retell the story without the use of the book and pictures, Chue had a much more difficult time. He would jump from one event to another without any type of transition. He used pronouns and syntax changes that did not help to clarify his thoughts for the listener. ("An then he jumped in the, she went in the water and got it for him. And he got in the basket and he, and her was scared.")

A tape-recorded language sample was obtained by having Chue tell the story of "Home Alone" (narrative) and talk about what he likes about school (conversation). The samples were obtained in English and in Hmong with the assistance of an interpreter. As there is no reference database for Hmong students at LEP Level 4, Language Sample Analysis was done by long hand. His mean length of utterances in morphemes (MLU) in English was 5.2 while his length in Hmong was approximately 6.0. A reduced number of words were used for his expressions in Hmong. His rate of speech was found to be very slow and labored. Many examples of formulation difficulties were noted with his tendency to have multiple pauses with and between utterances as well as syntactic word order errors. Although some syntactic errors are common for a student of Chue's age and background, he was found to not consistently use copular (is, are) and did not use "ing" verbing. Often articles were deleted (a, the). He also showed many examples of mazing and revisions at the word and phrase levels of expression (for example, "I, um, go downtown, uh, today. I like, uh, mall. Tomorrow no school. Uh, I like, uh, school, uh, sometimes. To draw is fun, Mr., uh, art teacher say I am very good. Um-um, I not know how to say word means hard to do." The interpreter indicated that he "jumps all over the place with his words." When trying to find the right word he would leave a word out, or revert to a blank stare and shrug his shoulders. In some cases, he would say that he didn't know the word. At times his pauses would be up to 4 seconds in length and he would appear to search for words.

On the Fisher Logemann Articulation Test, errors included -/s, -/z in the final positions of words. It must be noted, however, that the omission of these sounds is very characteristic of Hmong and should not necessarily be considered an articulation problem.

• a statement must be made regarding the modification of tests administered and the cultural implications
• specific vocabulary and concepts may not occur in the language
• morphological differences may be appropriate with the LCD population
• cultural differences may dictate pragmatic differences
• some articulation sound substitutions and omissions may be appropriate with the LCD population

Observations

Chue was observed in a variety of settings. In the classroom, he tended to be silent except when asked to be in a group discussion (this is characteristic of the Hmong culture). He only spoke when requested to answer a specific question. When called on, he appeared to need additional time to formulate his thoughts. When he did begin to respond verbally, his sentences were difficult to follow and contained many revisions and mazes. Chue would often talk all around a topic but could never get to the specific answer. However, he seemed to have a good understanding of what he had read, and remembered many of the details but could not specifically answer the question.

When observed playing with his peers, the same characteristics were noted. It appeared difficult to follow his conversations. He would be revising his thoughts and jumping from one topic to another without any type of transition.

• observe student in various settings (for example, classroom, ESL class, lunch room, and playground)
• observe (peer interaction, classroom teacher/child, Hmong interchanges, English usage, volunteering, and nonverbal communication)
• descriptive narratives give more accurate information than standardized tests that are biased against the culture and language of the Hmong population

Summary

Chue appeared to show difficulties in expressive language, most noted in his ability to formulate his thoughts into succinct verbal messages. Although his reticence to verbally participate within the classroom discussions could be culturally related, it does appear to be directly related to his expressive difficulties. His tendency to pause with many examples of mazes and word and phrase level revisions appear to be related to his formulation difficulties. He takes longer than average to retrieve the appropriate words to formulate his expressions.

It appears that at this particular time Chue is a Hmong student experiencing difficulties in the areas of verbal expression and sentence formulation. Background information, information from a Hmong-speaking interpreter, and current observations and formal testing suggest that Chue is experiencing the formulation difficulties in both languages and would benefit from inclusion in a speech and language program. It also is suggested that Chue be again involved in the ESL program with small group interactions and that verbal participation in the regular classroom is promoted and reinforced. Topics need to be provided in advance so that Chue can organize his thoughts.

8

Appendixes

General Comparisons: Black English and Standard American English

Standard American English Phonemes	Position in Word		
	Initial	Medial	Final*
/p/		Unaspirated /p/	Unaspirated /p/
	/n/		Reliance on
preceding			
			nazalized vowel
/w/	Omitted in specific words (*I'sas, too!*)		
/b/		Unreleased /b/	Unreleased /b/
/g/		Unreleased /g/	Unreleased/g/
/k/		Unaspirated /k/	Unaspirated /k/
/d/	Omitted in specific words (*I'on't know*)	Unreleased /d/	Unreleased /d/
/n/		/n/	/n/
/t/		Unaspirated /t/	Unaspirated /t/
/l/		Omitted before labial consonants (*help-hep*)	"uh" following a vowel (*Bill-Biuh*)
/r/		Omitted or /ə/	Omitted or prolonged vowel or glide
/Ø/	Unaspirated /t/ or /f/	Unaspirated /t/ or /f/ between vowels	Unaspirated /t/ or /f/ (*bath-baf*)
/v/	Sometimes /b/	/b/ before /m/ and /n/	Sometimes /b/
/ð/	/d/	/d/ or /v/ between vowels	/d/, /v/, /f/
/z/		Omitted or replaced by /d/ before nasal sound (*wasn't-wud'n*)	

Blends
/str/ becomes /skr/
/ʃ r/ becomes /str/
/θ r/ becomes /θ/
/pr/ becomes /p/
/br/ becomes /b/
/kr/ becomes /k/
/gr/ becomes /g/

Final Consonant Clusters (second consonant omitted when these clusters occur at the end of a word)
/sk/ /nd/ /sp/
/ft//ld/ /d₃ d/
/st/ /sd/ /nt/

---

*Note weakening of final consonants.
   Sources: Data drawn from Fasold and Wolfram (1970); Labov (1972); F. Weiner and Lewnau (1979); R. Williams and Wolfram (1977).

Black English	*Standard American English*
Grammatical Structure	*Grammatical Structure*

Possessive - 's
Nonobligatory where word
position expresses possession.
    Get mother coat.
    It be mother's.

Obligatory regardless of position.
    Get mother's coat.
    It's mothers.

Plural - s
Nonobligatory with numerical quantifer.
    He got ten *dollar*.
    Look at the cats.

Obligatory regardless of numerical quantifier.
    He has ten dollars
    Look at the cats.

Regular past - *ed*
    Nonobligatory; reduced as consonant
cluster.
    Yesterday, I *walk* to school.

Obligatory.
    Yesterday, I *walked* to school.

Irregular past
    Case by case, some verbs inflected,
others not.
    I *see* him last week.

All irregular verbs inflected.
    I *saw* him last week.

Regular present tense third person singular - *s*
    Nonobligatory.
    She *eat* too much.

Obligatory.
She *eats* too much.

Irregular present tense third persons ingular - *s*
    Nonobligatory.
    He *do* my job.

Obligatory.
    He *does* my job.

Indefinite *an*
    Use of indefinate *a*.

    He ride in *a* airplane.

Use of *an* before nouns beginning with
a vowel.
    He rode in *an* airplane.

Pronuns
    Pronominal apposition: pronoun
immediately follows noun.
    Momma *she* mad. She...

Pronoun used elsewhere in sentence or in
other sentence: not in apposition.
    Momma is mad. *She*...

Future tense
    More frequent use of *be going* to (goonna).
    I *be going* to dance tonight.
    I *gonna* dance tonight.
    Omit *will* preceding be.
    I *be* home later.

More frequent use of *will*.
I *will* dance tonight.
    I *am* going to dance tonight.
Obligatory use of *will*.
    I *will* (I'll) be home later.

Negation
    Triple negative.
    Nobody don't never like me.
    Use of *ain't*.
    I *ain't* going.

Absence of triple negative.
    No one ever likes me.
Ain't is unacceptable form.
    I'm *not* going.

Black English	Standard American English
Grammatical Structure	*Grammatical Structure*

Modals
Double modals for such forms as might, *could*, and *should*.
I *might* could go.

Single Modal use.
I *might be able* to go.

Questions
Same form for direct and indirect.
What *is it*?
Do you know what *it is*?

Different forms for direct and indirect.
What *is it*?
Do you know what *it is*?

Relative pronouns
Nonobligatory in most cases.
he the one stole it.
It the one you like.

Nonobligatory with *that* only.
He's the one *who* stole it.
It's the one (that) you like.

Conditional if
Use of *do* for conditinal if.
I ask *did* she go.

Use of *if*.
I asked *if* she went.

Perfect construction
Been used for action in the distant
past: He *been* gone.

Been not used: He left a long time ago.

Copula
Nonobligatory when contractible:
He sick.

Obligatory in contractible and uncontrac-
tible forms: He's sick.

Habitual or general state
Marked with uninflected *be*.
She *be* workin'.

Nonuse of *be*; verb inflected.
She's *working* now.

Sources: Data drawn from Baratz (1969), Fasold and Wolfram (1970), Williams and Wolfram (1977).

Hmong Resources

Educators seeking interpreters and aides may find help through existing resource directories, such as United Way, Community Chest, and other fund-raising organizations. Communities with large numbers of Hmong and non-Hmong refugees may have mutual assistance associations, and staff members at these organizations also may be of assistance.

Formal and informal leaders in the Hmong community also may provide help. Hmong families are organized along clan lines, and clan leaders (usually the eldest male of the clan family) are empowered to make decisions for the family. Clan leaders exert tremendous power over the lives of their family members. Solutions to any disputes or problems are usually sought within the clan family before outside help is considered.

Educators also may find assistance through local libraries, technical schools, or universities, which may offer English language programs and literacy classes for Hmong adults.

Evaluation Assistance Center-East
George Washington University
1730 N. Lynn St.
Arlington, VA 22209
(703) 528-3588
(800) 925-EACE
FAX: 703-528-5978

Department of Public Instruction
P.O. Box 7841
Madison, WI 53707
(608) 267-9234

National Origin Desegregation Project
Bureau for Equal Educational Opportunity
Department of Public Instruction
P.O. Box 7841
Madison, WI 53707
(608) 267-2283

Multifunctional Resource Center for Bilingual Education
Wisconsin Center for Educational Research
School of Education, UW-Madison
1025 Johnson St.
Madison, WI 53706
(608) 263-4220

Wisconsin Division of Health
Bureau of Community Health and Prevention
Family and Community Health Section
Refugee Health Program
P.O. Box 309
Madison, WI 53701-0309
(608) 266-9452

Refugee Assistance Office
Division of Community Services
Department of Health and Social Services
P.O. Box 7851
Madison, WI 53707
(608) 266-8354

University Film and Video
University of Minnesota
1313 5th St., S.E., Suite 108
Minneapolis, MN 55455
(612) 627-4270
(800) 847-8251

National Clearinghouse for Bilingual Education
George Washington University
1118 22nd St., NW
Washington, D.C. 20037
(202) 467-0867

(800) 321-NCBE
FAX: (202) 429-9766
A division of NCBE, Refugee Service Center, publishes In America, Perspectives on Refugee Resettlement, six times a year. It is available free of charge.

Southeast Asian Refugee Studies Project (SARS)
Center for Urban and Regional Affairs (CURA)
University of Minnesota
330 Hubert Humphrey Center
301 19th Ave., SE
Minneapolis, MN 55455
(612) 625-5535
The South Asian Refugee Studies Newsletter, published quarterly in January, April, July and October and other materials are available.

Bureau of Refugee Programs
1200 University Ave. Suite D
Des Moines, IA 50314
(800) 362-2780

Center for Southeast Asian Studies
104 Lane Hall
University of Michigan
Ann Arbor, MI 48106

Upper Great Lakes Multifunctional Resource Center
1025 W. Johnson St.
Madison, WI 53706
(608) 263-4220

Technical Assistance Center of the Southwest
Stephen F. Austin University
P.O. Box 13010A
SFA Station
Naccogdoches, TX 75962
A free catalog of audiovisual materials, including information on multicultural issues, refugees, and Indians, is available.

Ethnic and Multicultural Bulletin
The Council for Exceptional Children
1920 Association Dr.
Reston, VA 22091-1589
(703) 620-3660
FAX: (703) 264-9494

The Journal of Educational Issues of Language Minority Students
1910 University Dr.
Education Building 215
Boise State University
Boise, ID 83725
A referenced journal is published three times a year. Free copies available upon request.

Ethnotes
Joan Good Erickson, Editor
901 S. Sixth St.
Champaign, IL 61820
The format is designed to promote an exchange of ideas and resources between those professionals who share an interest in studying communication disorders from an ethnographic perspective. It is intended as a tool for networking members of the Ethnography in Communication Disorders (ECD) Interest Group, formally associated with the American Speech-Language-Hearing Association.

Multicultural Task Force
American Speech-Language-Hearing Association
10801 Rockville Pike
Rockville, MD 20852
(301) 897-5700

Wisconsin Speech-Language-Hearing Association
P.O. Box 1109
Madison, WI 53701
(800) 545-0640

National Association for the Advancement of Colored People (NAACP)
Social Development Commission (SDC)
3500 N. 26th St.
Milwaukee, WI 53206
(414) 871-1000

Wisconsin Educational Association Council
P.O. Box 8003
Madison, WI 53708-8003
Wisconsin Council for the Gifted and Talented
5912 Schumann Dr.
Madison, WI 53711-5103

Hmong Folk Tales and accompanying tapes and Hmong language materials are available for purchase from the following places.

Linguistics Department
Macalester College
St. Paul, MN 55105

Hmong Catholic Center
68 W. Exchange St.
St. Paul, MN 55102-1006

Center for Applied Linguistics
1118 22nd St., NW
Washington, D.C. 20037
(202) 429-9292

Hmong Volunteer Literacy Group
P.O. Box 56
Winfield, IL 60190

Hmong Tales
English/Hmong
Forest Home Ave. Library Branch
1432 W. Forest Home Ave.
Milwaukee, WI 53215

General Comparisons/Implications Between Hmong and English Languages

Phonology
Articulation differences
1. There are no final consonants in Hmong.
2. Hmong is a tonal language—every syllable is pronounced with one of seven tones. Meaning varies with tone shifts.
3. Sounds that occur in English but NOT in Hmong:
   Sound   th   th   e   a   z
   Phonetics
4. Possible articulation confusions that a Hmong child may have with English consonants.
   b, v, w   will be confused with each other
   z   will be confused with zh (i.e. measure)
   th   will be confused with t
   th   will be confused with d
   l, r   will be confused with each other
   p, b   will be confused with each other
   k, g   will be confused with each other
   t, d   will be confused with each other
   q   will sound more like k or g
5. Hmong words are almost always one syllable.
6. There are 32 consonant sounds in Hmong (22 in English).
7. There are six simple vowels in Hmong compared to 9 or 11 in English.
8. Initial and final consonant clusters will be difficult for the Hmong to pronounce.
9. "Breathiness" or aspiration is an important part of Hmong speech, especially on p, t, k, ch.

Structural Properties
Hmong is similar to English in the following ways.
1. A simple sentence will usually have a subject, verb and object.
2. Has prepositions used before noun objects.
3. Has helping verbs preceding main verb.
4. Constructs complex and compound sentences in similar ways.
Language differences occur in the following
   A. Word order
- adjectives and other modifiers follow rather than precede the nouns.
Implications: It will be more difficult to use an adjective before a noun, since it is the opposite order of their language.
- Questions are formed by adding question words, rather than by intonation or by changing the word order.
Implication: It is often necessary to rephrase questions
- There is no equivalent of the verb "be" before an adjective or adverb in Hmong (i.e. I happy. They here).
   B. Monosyllabic Words—Lexical Use of Tone
- Words are monosyllabic consisting of an initial sound followed by a vowel and a tone (8). Words differing in only tonal quality signify distinct meaning. In English, intonation is associated with a sentence.
- Hmong may attend to voice pitch as a lexical tone.
- Meaning carried in written English by punctuation and orally by intonation, is often carried by particles at the end of sentences in oral Hmong.
- English sarcasm and irony is conveyed with intonation along with gestures or facial expressions. If these other aspects are missed, the sarcastic intent is missed and the student will respond literally.

Translators and Interpreters

Most people use the terms interpreter and translator interchangeable; however, interpretation refers to oral communication and translation refers to written communication. Both interpreters and translators convert a message from one language to another.

The primary function of an interpreter is to make it possible for all those involved in an exchange of information to understand one another, despite language and cultural differences. The interpreter facilitates communication. A competent, knowledgeable interpreter is able to establish more direct communication, build trust, and reduce the possibility of the transmission of misinformation.

Therefore, the use of an interpreter who speaks the student's first language is crucial to the special education process when assessing students whose first language is not English. This also ensures that appropriate and legal methods have been followed throughout the assessment process and the risk of bias has been minimized as much as possible.

The Individuals with Disabilities Education Act (IDEA) states that a school district must "take whatever action is necessary to insure that the parent understand the proceedings at a meeting, including arranging for an interpreter for parents who are deaf or whose native language is other than English." (34 CFR 300.345). Because very few speech and language pathologists are qualified to provide a true bilingual assessment, they must rely on qualified and trained personnel to assist in the process.

It is best to choose an interpreter who is familiar with the process of educational assessment. If the interpreter has not received training, special education personnel must take the responsibility of training the person selected. The training must include the purpose of the process, the tasks involved, and expectations about the information to be gathered. Interpreters are expected to have

● the oral language proficiency and fluency to serve effectively in a variety of roles and to adjust to different levels of language use.

● the ability to relate to children from the particular cultural group with which they will be working.

● the ability to maintain confidentiality of school records and respect the rights of parents and students involved.

Ideally, interpreters should be able to read and write fluently in both languages. This allows them to supply parents with written communications, telephone parents to schedule meetings, and participate at M-team and other parent meetings with school personnel.

The five types of interpretation and translation are:

● consecutive interpretation: An interpreter listens to the message in the first language (L1), pauses for a moment, then converts the message into the second language (L2). Speakers need to keep sentences and information short and meaningful. This type of interpretation is usually used for parent conferences and testing situations.

● simultaneous interpretation: The interpreter gives an immediate interpretation of the message. Longer units of information must be recalled and synonyms used if applicable. This is very difficult and usually requires much training. United Nations' interpreters would be an example of this type of interpreter.

● whispered interpretation: During this event, the interpreter would sit beside the speaker and whisper interpretations as the meeting proceeds.

● prepared translation: Prior to the situation, the interpreter or translator is given time to review the material and prepare a written translation. Words can be clarified and questions asked ahead of the actual event.

● sight translation: A written translation is done at the time of the event.

In the educational setting, consecutive translation is most commonly used, although it is possible that a prepared translation may be necessary prior to a multidisciplinary team (M-team) and/or individualized educational program (IEP) meeting.

Training Interpreters and Translators

An interpreter who has received appropriate training in special education assessment processes and procedures can contribute much to an evaluation. The speech and language pathologist often is responsible for training an interpreter because the language component of the evaluation is such a vital link to the child's overall functioning.

Many English educational terms, especially special education terms, do not exist in other languages. The interpreter should be familiar with these terms and should not change the meaning of these terms during testing or conferences.

An interpreter training program should include

● knowledge of the terminology used in education and in assessment.

● knowledge of school personnel and their various roles within the school to help encourage mutual trust between school and family.

● information about remaining objective during interpretative exchanges, along with a sensitivity toward parents and students' rights and emotions.

● information about imparting cultural information to other professionals in order to help them learn more about the child's background.

● an understanding of the reasons for evaluation, knowledge of expectations, and rationale for tests used. This enables the interpreter to understand the procedures as well as to explain to a student the tasks being asked.

● knowledge of the laws, legal and ethical implications, and issues pertaining to the special education process.

● training in the multidisciplinary team (M-team) process, including roles and expectations.

● training in the importance of establishing rapport with the student.

● training in test administration procedures (for example, avoidance of prompting or commenting on the students' responses and stating questions exactly as possible within the limits imposed by the fact that some words are not translatable from one language to another).

● training to avoid giving non-verbal cues (for example, accompanying a question or statement with a gesture).

● training in the importance of the impact that non-verbal behaviors have on communication and the need to objectively and precisely report these behaviors.

Working with an Interpreter

Prior to assessment, the speech and language pathologist should:

● meet with the interpreter to discuss the nature of the assessment or conference so that both are aware of what is to be discussed.

● make a list of terms available to the interpreter and address any questions the interpreter may have.

● advise the interpreter of the importance of retaining the meaning of what is said and of not imposing their opinions or judgment into the communicative exchange.

● remind the interpreter of the need for confidentiality.

During the assessment, the speech and language pathologist should:

● keep statements brief—two to three sentences are enough at one time for an interpreter to remember and interpret.

● look at the parents or student, not at the interpreter. This interpreter is a vehicle for transmitting information—the parents and student are the people receiving the information. The SLP should never say, "Tell them." The SLP should tell them and the interpreter will interpret.

● have the interpreter sit beside the person who will do most of the talking during the exchange.

● speak normally, avoid "baby talk" but also avoid use of professional jargon that is difficult to interpret and will carry little meaning to the parents.

- never have a child interpret for his parents. This places the child in a very awkward position and could have negative cultural implications.
- be culturally sensitive and be aware that certain pressures may be placed upon the interpreter.

After the assessment, the speech and language pathologist should

- discuss what took place.
- ask the interpreter for subjective feedback. This feedback does not replace clinical judgment.
- include in the assessment report the use of the interpreter and his or her name.

For the interpreter

What are interpreters and translators? An interpreter or translator may speak, read, and write two or more languages and is able to convey the meaning of a conversation or dialog or written material from one language to another. The following guidelines provide a framework for interpreters and translators.

- Try to speak with the parents, guardians, and student before an assessment or conference to determine that the dialects are the same. If the interpreter or translator is familiar with the family, this may not be necessary.
- Explain to the student and family that during the assessment or conference the interpreter or translator is translating information even though at other times the interpreter or translator may be a friend or advocate.
- Discuss areas of concern to be covered at the meeting and agree upon terms to be communicated. This will avoid "inventing" terms on the spot.
- The interpreter or translator should sit beside the person who will do most of the talking at the meeting.
- One to three sentences should be the maximum before translation. The interpreter or translator may not remember an important point if too much is said at one time. The interpreter or translator should request clarification if he or she is confused.
- The interpreter or translator is not an editor. Everything that is said at an assessment or conference by parents, staff members, or the student must be translated. The interpreter or translator should use language that is most readily understood by the listener. The interpreter or translator should not counsel, advise, or add personal opinions.
- All information discussed at any school-related meeting is confidential. School-related information may be shared only among professionals working directly with students or the students' families.

Resources

Council for Exceptional Children. *Education of Culturally and Linguistically Different Exceptional Children*. Reston, VA: Council for Exceptional Children, 1984.

Diaz, J. *The Process and Procedures for Identifying Exceptional Language Minority Children*. College Station: Pennsylvania State University, 1988.

EauClaire School District. *Guidelines for Working with a Translator*. EauClaire, WI. EauClaire School District, 1992.

Madison Metropolitan School District. *Guidelines for Using a Foreign Language Translator*. Madison, WI: Madison Metropolitan School District, LEP Programs, working copy.

Test Evaluation Form

Title of Test:

Author:

Publisher:

Date of Publication:

Directions: Evaluate the test in each of the areas below using the following scoring system.
G = Good   F = Fair   P = Poor   NI = No Information   NA = Not Applicable

I. Purposes of the Test
_____ A. The purposes of the test are described adequately in the test manual.
_____ B. The purposes of the test are appropriate for the intended local uses of the instru
ment.
Comments:

II. Construction of the Test
_____ A. Test was developed based on a contemporary theoretical model of
speech-language development and reflects the findings of recent research.
_____ B. Procedures used in developing test content (e.g. selection and field-testing of test
items) were adequate.
Comments:

III. Prodecures
A. Procedures for test administration:
_____ 1. Described adequately in the test manual.
_____ 2. Appropriate for the local population.
B. Procedures for scoring the test:
_____ 1. Described adequately in the test manual.
_____ 2. Appropriate for the local population.
C. Procedures for test interpretation:
_____ 1. Described adequately in the test manual.
_____ 2. Appropriate for the local population.
Comments:

IV. Linguistic Appropriateness of the Test
_____ A. Directions presented to the child are written in the dialect used by the local
population.
_____ B. Test items are written in the dialect used by the local population.
Comments:

V. Cultural Appropriateness of the Test
_____ A. Types of tasks that the child is asked to perform are culturally appropriate for the local population.
_____ B. Content of test items is culturally appropriate for the local population.
_____ C. Visual stimuli (e.g. stimulus pictures used on the test) are culturally appropriate for the local population.
Comments:

VI. Adequacy of Norms
_____ A. Procedures for selection of the standardization sample are described in detail.
_____ B. Standardization sample is an appropriate comparison group for the local population in terms of:
     _____ 1. Age
     _____ 2. Ethnic background
     _____ 3. Place of birth
     _____ 4. Community of current residence
     _____ 5. Length of residency in the United States
     _____ 6. Socioeconomic level
     _____ 7. Language classification (e.g. limited English proficient)
     _____ 8. Language most often used by child at home
     _____ 9. Language most often used by child at school
     _____ 10. Type of language program provided in school setting (e.g. bilingual education)
Comments:

VII. Adequacy of Test Reliability Data
_____ A. Test-retest reliability
_____ B. Alternate form reliability
_____ C. Split-half or internal consistency
Comments:

VIII. Adequacy of Test Validity Data
_____ A. Face validity
_____ B. Content validity
_____ C. Construct validity
_____ E. Concurrent validity
_____ F. Predictive validity
Comments:

Checklist for Determination of Potential
Discrimination of an Assessment Instrument

(Reprinted with permission from "Culturally Valid Testing: A Proactive Approach" by Orlando L. Taylor and Kay T. Payne in *Topics of Language Disorders*, June 1983.)

1. Do I know the specific purpose for which this test was designed?
2. Has the test been validated for this purpose?
3. Are any limitations of the test described in the manual?
4. Do I know the specific information about the group on whom the test was standardized (sociocultural, sex, age, etc.)?
5. Are the characteristics of the student being tested comparable to those in the standardization sample?
6. Does the test manual or research literature (or my own experience) indicate any differences in test performance across cultural groups?
7. Do test items take into account differences in values or adaptive behaviors?
8. Does the test use vocabulary that is cultural, regional, colloquial, or archaic?
9. Does the test rely heavily on receptive and expressive standard English language to measure abilities other than language?
10. Is an equivalent form of the test available in any other language?
11. Am I aware of what the test demands of (or assumes about) the students in terms of:
    * reading level of questions or directions;
    * speech of response;
    * style of problem solving;
    * "test-taking" behaviors; and
    * format?
12. Will students with specific physical or sensory disabilities be penalized by this test or by certain items?
13. Has an item-by-item analysis been made of the test from the framework of the linguistic and communicative features of the group for which it is to be used?

Evaluation of Discrete-Point Test Used with Language Minority Children

Name of test _____

Publication year _____

Normative population _____

Validity data _____

Reliability data _____

Strengths and weaknesses for use with minority children

Alternative Scoring Analysis

Test Item	Standard Response	BEV Alternative	L2 Learning Alternative	Influence on Score

Classroom Observation Form

(Adapted from *Bilingual Special Education* by Leonard M. Baca and Hermes T. Cervantes. Reston, VA: Council for Exceptional Children, 1988.)

Student name: _____ Date of observation: _____

School: _____ Grade: _____

Teacher name: _____ Observer: _____

Classroom Setting: (Include approximate number of students, seating, organization of classroom, time of day, etc.)

Specific Activity:

Management/Instructional Techniques of Teacher: (Include use of positive or negative reinforcement, verbal and non-verbal cues, teacher-child interactions, materials presented, use of questions, types of directions, etc.)

Student's Behavior with Independent Seat Work: (Include attending to task, amount of work completed, comparison to peers, need for assistance, etc.)

Student's Behavior in Groups: (Include group size, types of interactions between student and other group members, etc.)

Student's Interactions with Peers in Classroom Setting: (Include how conversations are initiated, by whom, responses of student, etc.)

Additional Comments:

Does the teacher believe that the student's behavior during the observation period was typical of his or her everyday performance?

Classroom Teacher Questions for Self-Evaluation Prior to Making a Referral

These questions may help a classroom teacher evaluate possible sources of bias prior to referring a student. They will also help to analyze and focus on the needs of the student .

1. What special factors about myself do I need to consider?
2. How do I feel about this child?
3. Are my values different from this child's?
4. Can I assess this child fairly and without prejudice?
5. Have I examined closely all of the available existing information and sought additional information concerning this child?
6. Have I observed this child in as many environments as possible (individual, large group, small group, play, home)?
7. Am I making illegitimate assumptions about this child (e.g., Have I assumed he speaks and reads Hmong because he is Southeast Asian? Have I assumed he has less ability because he may be less verbal than mainstream children?)?
8. Have I been able to resolve non-school related variables that may affect this child's school performance? Are there health factors (sleep, nutrition), family issues (homelessness, divorce, death), or peer group issues that should be considered?
9. Is the parent(s)/guardian(s) aware that I am concerned about their child?
10. Am I able to clearly and precisely state my concerns about this child?

Communication Skills Inventory for Bilingual Children

(Adapted from *Speech and Language Assessment for the Bilingual Handicapped* by L. Mattes and D. Omark. San Diego, CA: College Hill Press, 1984.)

This form can be completed by classroom teachers, speech/language pathologists, bilingual education teachers or aides, or English as a Second Language teachers. The responses should be interpreted in view of communication behaviors that are typical or appropriate for individuals from the student's culture.

Child's Name: _____ Date of Birth: _____

Child's First Language: _____ Child's Second Language: _____

Completed by: _____

Communicative Behavior	First Language	Second Language
Comments on own actions		
Comments on others' actions		
Describes experiences accurately		
Describes events sequentially		
Attends to the speaker		
Follows directions		
Initiates interactions		
Takes turns during conversation		
Maintains topic		
Answers questions		
Requests attention		
Requests information		
Requests action		
Requests clarification		
Expresses needs		
Expresses feelings		
Describes plans		
Supports viewpoints		
Describes solutions		
Expresses imagination		

Consultation Team Questionnaire for use with Students from Linguistically and Culturally Diverse Backgrounds

	Yes	No
The school environment appears to be culturally sensitive.		
Culturally and linguistically diverse families are involved in the school.		
The classroom appears to reflect a culturally sensitive environment.		
Large class size affects whether the teacher can individualize instruction or try alternative methods of instruction.		
The language of instruction matches the student's (complexity, dominant language, dialect, and so forth).		
The teacher refers students from this culture appropriately.		
Instruction provides a. Varied methods of instruction b. Modified curriculum c. Varied management		
Modifications were made to meet the needs of the student.		
The curriculum matches the level of instruction needed by the child.		
The curriculum does not match the instructional level of the student, but modifications can be made.		
Someone from the school or district has had contact with the family.		
A translator who speaks the child's native language has been located.		
There is a professional on the team who can speak to the issues of linguistic and cultural differences (for example, a cultural representative).		

Records Review Form

(Adapted from *A Resource Handbook for the Assessment and Identification of LEP Students with Special Education Needs*. White Bear Lake, MN: Minnesota Services Center, 1987.)

School Experience

Country outside of the United States (Circle each grade completed)

K   1   2   3   4   5   6   7   8   9   10   11   12

United States (Circle each grade completed)

K   1   2   3   4   5   6   7   8   9   10   11   12

Retained: YES   NO

Attendance: GOOD   POOR   UNKNOWN

Number of Days Absent: _____

Other schools attended outside of local school district: _____

Last school attended: _____

Have records been obtained from former school district? _____ YES   _____ NO

Has the child been advanced a grade? _____ YES   _____ NO

When and at what grade? _____

Program Placements (Circle all that apply)

Regular Education	PreK	K	1	2	3	4	5	6	7	8	9	10	11	12
Bilingual Education	PreK	K	1	2	3	4	5	6	7	8	9	10	11	12
Chapter 1	PreK	K	1	2	3	4	5	6	7	8	9	10	11	12
	PreK	K	1	2	3	4	5	6	7	8	9	10	11	12

Special Education

Disability_____	PreK	K	1	2	3	4	5	6	7	8	9	10	11	12
Disability _____	PreK	K	1	2	3	4	5	6	7	8	9	10	11	12
Disability _____	PreK	K	1	2	3	4	5	6	7	8	9	10	11	12
Social Work	PreK	K	1	2	3	4	5	6	7	8	9	10	11	12
Counseling	PreK	K	1	2	3	4	5	6	7	8	9	10	11	12
Other_____	PreK	K	1	2	3	4	5	6	7	8	9	10	11	12

Previous Testing and/or Screening Data:

Date: _____   Test: _____   Results: _____
Date: _____   Test: _____   Results: _____
Date: _____   Test: _____   Results: _____
Date: _____   Test: _____   Results: _____

Teacher Interview for Consultation Team

Child's Name: _____   Teacher's Name: _____

Interviewed by: _____

	Yes	No
Is the child's functioning consistent across settings and skills? Comments:		
Have samples of academic performance been collected over time? (Attach) Comments:		
Is the child's functioning showing improvement over time? Comments:		
Has the child's academic performance been consistent from year to year? Comments:		
Is there evidence in records that performance was negatively or positively affected by classroom placement or teacher? Comments:		
Are past test scores consistent with past class performance? Comments:		
Are you familiar with past test instruments used to evaluate the child? Can the prior test scores be interpreted reliably? Comments:		
Is there evidence of a disability other than the referral problem that may result in a language comprehension problem? Comments:		
Has the child been receiving ESL services? Comments:		
Has information been obtained from former school districts? Comments:		
Has the child been advanced a grade? When? What grade? Comments:		
Has the child been retained? When? What grade? Comments:		
Does the child understand in English: A. Words B. Phrases C. Sentences D. Conversations Comments:		
Does the child converse in another language? Another dialect? Comments:		

	Yes	No
Is the child difficult to understand In English? In his or her native language? Comments:		
Does the child have difficulty communicating with peers A. In English? B. In his or her native language? Comments:		
Can the child describe events sequentially? Comments:		
Does the child demonstrate appropriate listening behavior? Comments:		
Is the child able to follow oral directions presented in the classroom? Comments:		
Does the child stop and search for words ? Comments:		
Does the child code switch in conversation? Comments:		
Is the child's syntax/word order appropriate? Comments:		
Is there a difference between the child's oral work and written work? Comments:		
What are the child's strengths? Comments:		
What are the child's greatest weaknesses at this time? Comments:		
How does the student compare to peers of the same cultural background? Comments:		
Is the child able to stay on task? Comment:		
Does the child verbally interact in classroom discussions? Comments:		
Does the child verbally interact with peers in informal activities? Comments:		

Sample Interview Form

Educators should use this form when interviewing parents or caregivers concerning a student's home functioning.

Date: _____ Ethnic Code: _____ Birthdate _____ Age _____

Student Name: _____ ID: _____

Address: _____

Phone: _____ School: _____

Parents/Guardians: _____

1. Tell me about (name).
2. Describe for me what you remember when (name) was beginning to talk.
   Was (his or her) speech easy to understand?
3. When (name) talked, did (his or her) speech sound like the other children in the family?
   (if not) Describe how it was different?
4. Did (name) sound like the children in the neighborhood?
   (if not) Describe how it was different?
5. Once (name) had established a pattern of talking, did you notice a change in the way
   (name) used language, or the patterning of the language? In other words, did (name)
   sound more like you or the neighborhood playmates? At about what age or in what setting
   was the pattern of language different?
6. Describe the way (name) talked at first and how (name) talks now.
7. Has (name) always lived with you? Have you always been the primary caretaker?
   (if no) Does (name) sound more like you or others who care for (him or her)
   Explain a little about the way some of the other people who were often around (name)
   spoke to (him or her)
8. Pragmatic Behavior
   a. When you engage in a conversation with (name) is there turntaking? Does (name) like
      to talk, or does (name) use a lot of gestures, such as hand or facial expressions rather
      than words or sentences? Describe a common event where (name) would feel comfort-
      able enough to express (himself or herself) freely?
   b. Does (name) usually wait until you have finished your statement before responding?
   c. Do (name's) playmates seem to like to talk with (him or her)?
   d. Tell me about the best time for talking at home. Who talks with (name) the most at
      home?
   e. Describe the kind of punishment that is used when (name) does not listen. Who usually
      does the punishment?
   f. Do you encourage (name) to speak the language structure that is taught in school by
      the teachers, or do you prefer that (name) talk like (his or her) friends in the neighbor-
      hood? What would you like to see change?
   g. Does (name) seem to learn quickly, or does it take many repeated exposures for (him or
      her) to learn?

Comments: (The speech and language pathologist should describe the linguistic pattern of
the person interviewed.)

Background Information on Students with Limited-English Proficiency

Date: _____

Person completing form:

Information obtained from:

Other people present:

1. Identifying information

Name of child: Sex: Male   Femae

Date of birth: Place of birth:

Address:

Phone:

Parents (or other person's with whom student lives—relationship):

Cultural group (Hmong, Laotian, etc.):

Primary language spoken at home:

Arrival in United States:

Length of time in refugee camp (if applicable):

Person to contact for school-related matters:

How long has family lived in local community:

Father's occupation:

Last grade of school attended:

Mother's occupation:

Last grade of school attended:

What language/languages do parents speak, understand, read, write?

Siblings:

Name	Age	Grade	Relevant Information

Do or did any members of your immediate or extended family have learning, speech, or hearing difficulties that may affect the child's school experience? ____ yes ____ no

    If yes, explain:

2. Developmental History (If known)

Pregnancy with this child: Normal _____ Problems _____
   If problems, explain:

Length of pregnancy: _____ months

Length of active labor was: ____ under 3 hours ____ 3 to 24 hours ____ over 24 hours

Was infant premature: ____ yes _____ no
   If so, how early?

Which word best describes your child's prenatal activity level?
   ____Quiet _____ Active _____ Overactive

Birth weight: _____ pounds ____ ounces

Type of delivery: _____ Natural _____ Caesarean Section

Was infant born: _____ head first ____ feet first ____ breech

Was it necessary to give the infant oxygen? ____ yes ____ no
   If so, for how long?

Did infant require any special treatments (for example, blood transfusion, x-ray, EEG)?
   If so, explain:

Did infant appear yellow (jaundiced): _____ yes _____ no

Did infant have breathing difficulties: _____ yes ____ no

Did infant have:
   _____ Convulsions or twitching   _____ Prolonged vomiting
   _____ Feeding difficulty   _____ Prolonged high fever
   _____ Prolonged irritability
   If yes, to any questions, please explain:

Was infant slow in responding: _____ yes _____ no

As an infant this baby was: ____ overactive ____ quiet ____ irritable _____ average

Did infant: _____ sleep well _____ sleep very little ____ never napped _____ sleep restlessly

Did infant have feeding difficulties? ____ yes ____ no
   If yes, explain:

Were patterns similar to your other children? ____ yes ____ no
   If no, explain:

At what age did child: _____sit alone _____crawl ____walk by him/herself
   ____feed him/herself ____say first words ____begin to put 2 and 3 words together

Is child's speech easily understood by family members? __ yes ____ no
   by others? _____ yes ____no
   If no, explain:

Compare his/her development to your other children:

3. Medical History

Did child suffer any serious illnesses? _____ yes _____ no
   If yes, explain:
Was child ever hospitalized? _____ yes _____ no
   If yes, explain:
   For how long? _____ At what age? _____

Did child ever have high fevers? _____ yes _____ no
   If yes, how long?
   Explain:

Did child ever experience convulsions? _____ yes _____ no
   If yes, with high fever: _____ yes _____ no
   with accident: _____ yes _____ no _____ no apparent cause

Did child have any accidents? _____ yes _____ no
   Been unconscious: _____ yes _____ no
   If yes, describe:

Is child on any type of medications? _____ yes _____ no
   If yes, for what reason:
   List drug, dosage, and problems, if any:

Has child had any hearing difficulties? _____ yes _____ no
   If yes, describe:

Has child had any ear infections? _____ yes _____ no
   If yes, please indicate when they occurred, number, length of time and treatments

Has child ever had a hearing evaluation? _____ yes _____ no
   If so, where and what were the results?

Has child had any visual problems? _____ yes _____ no
   If yes, explain:

Has child had a vision test? _____ yes _____ no
   If yes, when, where and what were the results?

Does child wear glasses? _____ yes _____ no

What doctors and agencies have worked with this child?
   Agency/person/service   phone   city   state

4. Speech and Language

What language did your child learn when he/she first began to talk?

Is your child difficult to understand in his/her native (first) language? Explain:

Do you feel your child understands what you say? ____ yes ____ no

What language does your child speak when he/she answers you?

What language(s) do parents speak to each other?

What language(s) do parents speak to the child?

What language(s) do the children use with each other?

What language does the child prefer to use when playing with friends?

Has child experienced some language loss in his/her first language? ____ yes ____ no   If yes, explain?

What language is used in ceremony services (church or traditional ceremonies, funerals, new births, weddings) if attended?

How much contact does the family have with the homeland? What kind of contact?

List any circumstances that would have deterred or influenced your child's development (for example, living in a refugee camp, numerous moves).

5. Social development

Who takes care of child after school?
  What language is used?

With whom does the child play?
  _____ older children
  _____ children the same age
  _____ adults
  _____ younger children
  _____ prefers to play alone

What are child's favorite activities, games, toys etc.?

What does child do after school and on weekends?

Are stories read to the child? ____ yes ____ no
  If yes, in what language?

Are stories told to the child? ____ yes ____ no
  If yes, in what language?

Can child tell a story back to you? ____ yes ____ no

Does your child watch T.V.? ____ yes ____ no
  How much time does child watch T.V.?

What responsibilities does the child have at home?

In what cultural activities does the family participate?

Hearing Screening for Southeast Asian Students

It is critical for all students with speech and language delays to have their hearing screened. This is especially important for southeast Asian students who are learning English as a second language. Subjectively it is difficult to assess if a language delay is due to learning a second language, a language disorder, or possibly a hearing loss. It is difficult to solely use input of parents and family members who may indicate that their child receptively and expressively communicates in his or her native language. Even a mild to moderate hearing loss can be deceiving, and it may be difficult to determine if a child hears if he or she is turned when their name was called or seems to hear. This is especially important if the native language is a "vocal" (for example, Hmong or Spanish) language with most word understanding depending on lower frequency consonants and vowels. If this same child possesses a congenital high frequency hearing loss he or she most likely will prefer their native language and will have difficulty with the English language, which depends on high frequency phonemes to carry the understanding of words (Abreu, 1995). This is often deceiving to family members and school personnel.

There are an estimated 8 million children throughout North America who have some degree of hearing loss (Berg, 1986). This represents one in every six children (16 percent). A higher incidence of hearing loss has been noted in the southeast Asian population (Nsouli, 1995; Bylander, 1985; Buchanan, et al., 1993). Data gathered from the Wausau School District indicates that in a three-year time frame, approximately 30 percent of southeast Asian students have failed routine hearing screenings. This is significant because routine follow-up is difficult due to cultural views and lack of understanding of American medicine.

A community with a large southeast Asian population may also have a high incidence of amplification use (hearing aids, FM units, classroom amplification) due to refusal of surgical procedures to correct conductive hearing losses. Parents also may refuse hearing aid use at home due to cultural views.

The educational audiologist is a critical resource in all school districts, especially if there is a large southeast Asian population. The educational audiologist's role is essential in providing assessment, inservices to teachers regarding classroom recommendations and expectations, hearing aid monitoring and fitting of FM units (Code of Federal Regulations, Chapter 32, 300.303; WI), acting as a liaison between the medical and educational environment, and so forth. The educational audiologist is the professional qualified by training and education to provide these services. The extent of the educational audiologist's involvement in working with southeast Asian students will vary depending upon the number of students enrolled in a school district and experience of others with providing needed screening and timely follow-up for these students.

A protocol such as the *Wisconsin Guide to Childhood Hearing Screening* is helpful to educational audiologists providing hearing screenings and follow-up. The following are other suggestions for providing hearing screenings for southeast Asian students.

● Otoscopic exam. This is essential in assessing cerumen build-up and/or eardrum abnormalities. Eardrums are often difficult to view due to dry or flaky cerumen.

● Tympanometry. Because a higher incidence of hearing loss exists in this population and follow-up is difficult, early detection and monitoring is important to ensure follow-up is provided quickly. Because many eardrums are difficult to view, tympanometry can help determine any abnormalities, such as a perforation. In a three-year time frame in the Wausau School District, a large number of southeast Asian students presented with type A (limited mobility) tympanograms and normal pure tone sensitivity. It is important that these students are monitored and not over-referred.

● Pure tone testing. Conditioned play audiometry has been very successful in testing southeast Asian children younger than 5 years old. An interpreter is seldom used and accurate results are easily obtained. The time frame to condition a child to raise his or her hand often takes longer and results are not as reliable.

If a child passes his or her pure tones, but fails the tympanograms, a recheck in four to six weeks is suggested. If a student fails, a translated letter should be sent home. The same day, an interpreter also should call home to inform the parents about the letter and what it means. The audiologist should instruct the parents to take the letter to their doctor. The family may need help with finding a physician, setting an appointment, and getting an interpreter.

Resources

Abreu, R. "Mainstreaming Bilingual Children with Hearing Loss." *Hearing Instruments*, August 1995, p. 9.

Berg, F.S. "Characteristics of the Target Population." In *Educational Audiology for the Hard of Hearing Child*. Eds F.S. Berg, J.C. Blair, H.H. Viehweg, and A. Wilson-Voltman. New York: Grune and Stratton, 1986.

Buchanan, L.H., E.J. Moore, and A.S. Counter. "Hearing Disorders and Auditory Assessment." In *Communication Disorders in Multicultural Populations,* Butterworth/Heinemann, 1993.

Bylander, A.K.H. "Influence of Age, Sex and Race on Eustachian Tube Function." *Ann Oto Rhinol Laryngol*. 94 (Suppl 12), pp. 28-39.

Nsouli, R. "Serious Otitis Media." *The Immuno Review* (Winter, 1995), vol. 3, pp. 2-7.

Wisconsin Department of Public Instruction. *The Wisconsin Guide to Childhood Hearing Screening*. Madison, WI: Wisconsin Department of Public Instruction, 1993.

Instructions for Performing the Audiometric Pure-Tone Hearing Rescreening Test

(Reprinted with permission from *The Wisconsin Guide to Childhood Hearing Screening*. Madison, WI: Wisconsin Department of Public Instruction, 1993.)

Selecting the Test Environment

A quiet test environment is absolutely essential. A room is quiet enough if the test tones can be heard easily by a person with normal hearing. If the tester's hearing is not normal, locate a young adult with no history of hearing problems to listen to the test tones. Do not proceed with the rescreening if all the test tones cannot be heard easily. The room noise sources must be located and reduced or a quieter room must be found if the test tones cannot be heard easily.

Audiometer Performance Check

The audiometer should be set to a loudness of 60 HL and a frequency of 2,000 Hz and set to "normally on" to determine that the tones reaching both earphones are steady (no static or interruptions). This should be done while you wiggle the earphone wires of each earphone at both ends. If any interruption of the tone is heard, do not proceed with the rescreening until the audiometer is repaired. Next, without changing the settings of the audiometer, move the ear selector switch back and forth between "left and right." The tone should be equally loud in both ears if the listener's hearing is normal and if the audiometer is working properly.

Instructions to the Child

The tester's instructions to the child should be simple and clear so that he or she knows exactly what is expected of him or her.
1. Explain that the tones will be soft and may be difficult to hear.
2. Seat the child facing 45 degrees away from the tester so that the tester can observe the child's reactions and so that the child cannot see the tester operating the audiometer.
3. Have the child place his or her hand on his or her knee while waiting for the tone.

4. Instruct the child to raise his or her hand every time he or she hears the tone, even if it is very soft and difficult to hear.
5. Instruct the child to raise his or her hand right away as soon he or she hears the tone.
6. Instruct the child to return his or her hand to his or her knee when the tone stops.
7. Be sure the child knows to which ear the tone will be presented.

When the Child is Ready for Screening
1. Expand the headband and place the red earphone on the right ear, the blue earphone on the left ear.
2. The tester should make certain that the opening in the center of the earphone is in direct line with the ear canal. Place the earphones on the child while facing him or her.
3. Adjust the earphones to the approximate size of the child's head before placing them in position. The headband should rest squarely in the center of the head.
4. Let the child know how he or she is doing. Praise him or her if he or she is doing well and reinstruct him or her if he or she is having difficulty with the task.

Demonstration Techniques
It may be necessary to demonstrate the test for some children who do not respond to the tones.
Pass/Fail and Referral Criteria
1. The frequencies of 1,000 Hz, 2,000 Hz, and 4,000 Hz should be used.
2. The audiometer loudness will be set to 20 dB HL for 1,000 and 2,000 Hz and 25 dB HL for 4,000.
3. The child must respond two out of three times to pass each frequency in each ear.
4. If the child passes at 1,000 or 2,000 Hz but fails at 4,000 Hz in either ear, then test 3,000 Hz at 20 dB HL in that ear.
5. Failure at 1,000 or 2,000 Hz in either ear is a rescreening failure. Failure at 4,000 Hz only in either or both ears is not a failure but will require a retest next year.
6. Failure at 3,000 AND 4,000 Hz in either or both ears is a rescreening failure.

Verifying the Failure
There are causes other than hearing loss for failure on the rescreening test. It is the tester's job to rule out these causes before accepting the failure. If a child fails any frequency in either ear.
1. Reposition the earphones and rescreen. The center of the earphone must be directly over the opening of the ear canal.
2. Increase the loudness of the tone failed to 60 dB HL to be sure the child understands the task and is paying attention. When it is clear that the child is paying attention and understands the task, reduce the loudness to the screening level and retest. If the child does not understand or is not paying attention, proceed to number three below.
3. Reinstruct the child, and remind him or her that the tones are soft. If necessary, remove the earphones and repeat the demonstration activity. Be generous with your praise for correct responding.
4. If a child cannot learn the screening task and does not respond to any 60 dB sounds, report him or her to the person in charge at your hearing screening program.

Referrals
Parents of children who fail the rescreening test should be informed of the failure and should be encouraged to obtain medical and audiological evaluations for their children. It is important that hearing screening personnel seek the results of the medical and audiological evaluations. If the hearing loss does not resolve with medical treatment, the child's school should be made aware of the problem. Periodic rescreening of children referred for medical evaluations and treatment is important to document the resolution of temporary hearing losses and the persistence of other hearing losses.

Annotated Coding Sample: Fifth-grade Female

Frog on his own: tell condition
Introduction
- Once there was a boy.
- [Um he took] he took his frog, his turtle and his dog to the park.
- And they went to the park
- [and] but [the frog] the frog got curious
- and he jumped out of the pail that [h] the boy was carrying the turtle and the frog in.
- And so [the] the boy, the dog, and the turtle went on
- but the frog stayed behind.

[Annotation: The Introduction is transcribed, but the propositions are not included in the story grammar analysis.]

Episode 1: The Bee

S	1	Then [the frog saw] the frog looked at flowers.
IE	2	And then he saw something buzzing in the flowers
AS	3	so he stuck out his tongue
AS	4	and licked the thing.
AS	5	When he licked it,
C	6	it stung the frog.
AS	7	So the frog spit [the] the thing out
S	8	and it was a bee.
S	9	The bee put a big lump [on the] on the frog's tongue
J	10	and the frog didn't have a good time.

[Annotation: In this episode, there is a clear Initiating Event (IE) (Line 2), followed by several Action Statements (AS) and a Consequence (C)(Line 6) of those actions. However, the episode lacks clear motive and planfulness as well as true intentional causality between events. On the basis of an Initiating Event + a Consequence, this episode is coded as a Level IV Abbreviated Episode. It is important to note that Settings (S) relate to initial introduction of the main character (line 1) as well as to introduction of a new character (Line 8) and changes in the main character's state (Line 9). In addition, the Judgment (J) (Line 10) reflects the narrator stepping out of her narrator's role and commenting on events in the story.]

Episode 2: The Picnic

IE	1	Then the frog saw the lady and a man having a picnic.
IR	2	And he wanted to know what was inside the picnic basket
A	3	so he helped himself go into the picnic basket.
A	4	Then the lady reached in for something
A	5	[and when he reach] and when she reached for something,
C	6	she felt something slimy and wet.
AS	7	So [she] she pulled her hand out.
C	8	But then [there] the frog was around her arm
AS	9	and she screamed.
AS	10	The man dropped his cup
AS	11	and [his glasses] his glasses fell off his eyes.
AS	12	And then the woman got all wet by coffee.
AS	13	And [the frog] she shouted [at the f] at the frog
AS	14	and the frog jumped off.
AS	15	But the man started laughing like crazy.

[Annotation: In this episode, there is clear evidence of intentionality on the part of both the frog and the lady. Actions occur purposefully, with true causal relationships between events.

An Initiating Event (IE) (Line 1) sets the stage for future planful behavior by both characters. The frog's Internal Response (IR) (Line 2) establishes his motive, which he acts on with
an Attempt (A) (Line 3). The lady's motive is implied, but her Attempt (A) (Lines 4 and 5) is
clearly stated. The Consequence (C) (Line 6) applies to both the frog and the lady, and the
lady's attempt has an additional Consequence (C) (Line 7) as well. This episode is coded as a
Level VII Interactive Episode because it reflects Complete Episode structures (IE + IR + A +
C) from both the frog and the lady's perspectives.]

Episode 3: The Sailboat

IE	1	Then the frog saw a boy playing with a boat [by the] by the lake.
IR	2	And he was very curious
A	3	so he jumped right on to [the] the little sailboat
C	4	and it sunk
R	5	and the little boy got mad.
AS	6	Then he cried
AS	7	and his mother who was sitting on the bench had to come and get the boat for him.
R	8	The frog got scared

[Annotation: In this episode, there is clear evidence of the frog's motive as well as a weak
causal relationship between events. An Initiating Event (IE) (Line 1) sets the stage for the
frog's Internal Response (IR) (Line 2). His Attempt (A) (Line 3) leads to a Consequence (C)
(Line 4) as well as the boy's Reaction (R) (Line 5). Although there is a direct relationship between the Attempt and the Consequence, the cause element is weak because the frog did not
intend to sink the boat; he was merely curious. This episode is coded as a Level V Complete
Episode because it contains elements required for such an episode (IE + IR + A + C) as well
as a weak causal relationship. It is important to note that the Response element (Line 8)
does not influence story grammar structure level. In addition, it relates to feelings or
thoughts rather than to actions.

Episode 4: The Baby in the Carriage

AS	1	and [when he got the frog got scared and] when he got [to the other side of the] the other side of the pond,
IE	2	he saw a lady and a cat in a carriage.
IR	3	He wanted to know what was inside of the carriage
A	4	so he jumped
C	5	and went right into the carriage.
AS	6	The cat saw
S	7	but the mother was busy reading on the bench.
AS	8	When the mother gave the baby the bottle
AS	9	the frog jumped right up
AS	10	and [the mother] instead the mother put it [into] right into the frog's mouth.
R	11	[The baby] the baby got mad
AS	12	and he started crying.

[Annotation: In this episode, an Initiating Event (IE) (Line 2) triggers the frog's Internal Response (IR) (Line 3) which, in turn, leads to his attempt (A) (Line 4) and its Consequence (C)
(Line 5). This episode is coded as a Level V Complete Episode because of the pattern reflected
in the propositions as well as the frog's clear intentionality.

Episode 5: The Cat

S   1   The cat saw the frog

AS   2   and the cat jumped right on top of the frog.

S   3   The lady saw the frog

AS   4   and she started to scream.

AS   5   Then she picked up her baby

AS   6   and the cat ran after the frog.

AS   7   The cat jumped on the frog

R   8   and he was sad that he was going to [loss his life] lose his life.

[Annotation: In this episode, there is no evidence of planfulness or purposeful behavior. The propositions represent a chronological listing of actions in temporal order but without indicating intentionality or causal relationships. Consequently, this episode is coded as a Level II Action Sequence.]

Conclusion

- But then the cat saw something
- and it was the dog.
- And the dog scared her away back to where she was.
- And then the boy told the dog to scare the cat away.
- And then the turtle saw the frog
- and [the] the boy put the frog in the pail again
- and [they walked] they walked home.

[Annotation: As with the Introduction, the Conclusion is transcribed, but the propositions are not included in the story grammar analysis.]

story grammar structure score: (4 + 7 + 5 + 5 + 2) = 23

Glossary

Academic Achievement: How well a student is learning in school.

Adaptive Behavior: Ability to cooperate and work with others.

ADD/ADHD Attention Deficit Disorder/Attention Deficit Hyperactivity Disorder: Difficulty paying attention.

Advisor: A person who helps you.

Alternative M-team Report: Report written by a person or persons of the M-team who do not agree with the findings of the rest of the M-team members.

Assessment and Evaluation: Information on the student from observation and testing.

Autism: A medical condition in which an individual has difficulty communicating or relating to others.

Bilingual: A person who has skills in two languages, although not necessarily equal for both languages.

Bilingual Instruction: A program of instruction for children of limited English where there is instruction in English and in the child's native language.

Bilingualism:

Additive: A process by which an individual learns a second language after or while developing their first language.

Limited: Individual has social communication in the two languages, but does not have the academic skills in either language.

Proficient: Individual has native-like ability to understand, speak, read, and write in two languages.

Subtractive: Learning of the native language is interrupted and the individual has poor proficiency or complete loss of their native language.

Case Manager: When a student is referred for testing the case manager gets the people who did the testing, the parent/guardian, and others together to share information and discuss what is best for the student.

Classroom Observation: What has been seen in the classroom.

Chapter I: A program in which the teacher provides extra help in reading or math.

Code Switching: Changing from one language to the other during conversation.

Cognitive: Ability.

Cognitive Delay (CD): Students who learn at a slower rate than their peers.

Consent for Evaluation: Permission to test.

Decision Making Process: Decide what to do.

Delivery Model: How the help will be provided—in the classroom, in a different room, and so forth.

Director or Designee: Person who looks at the information and along with the placement group makes the formal decision where the student is to be placed.

Discontinuation of Support Services: The end of extra help because the student no longer needs it.

Due Process Hearing: A legal way to make sure that a child's educational needs are being met. Can be used by the parents or school.

Educational Outcome: The goal of where you hope the student will be.

Emotionally Disturbed (ED): Children who have a hard time following rules which makes it more difficult to learn in the classroom.

English as a Second Language (ESL): Program that teaches English to students whose native language is not English.

Exceptional Educational Need (EEN): The student has difficulty learning because of delays or difficulty with language, hearing, behavior, learning, or motor skills.

FES/Fluent English-speaking: English is adequate to function in a regular English speaking classroom.

Handicapping Condition: See EEN

Hearing Impaired: Program in which children get different amounts of help from a hearing impaired teacher depending on the hearing loss they have.

Hmong:

Hmong Leng/Green Hmong: A dialect spoken by the Hmong people

White/Black Hmong: A dialect spoken by the Hmong people.

Home Language: Language spoken at home, in contrast with another language used in other situations.

Immunization: Shots given to prevent disease.

Individual Education Plan (IEP): Developed by a team or committee to address the present level of performance by the student, annual goals, and short term objectives.

I-94: Immigration and Naturalization Service I-94 alien registration card gives a legal "refugee" status to refugee arrivals and to those who have been in the U.S. a specified time.

Intervention Strategies: Different ways of teaching that are tried in order to give the student success.

Language:

Conversational: Language used to communicate socially.

Academic: Language skills needed for understanding and success in school.

Language Dominance: The language used with most ease.

L1/First Language: The language learned first when acquiring language.

L2/Second Language: The language learned second.

LD/Learning Disabilities: Individuals who have average ability but who have difficulty achieving in one or more of the major academic areas: i.e. math, reading, spelling. A learning disability teacher helps them with learning.

LEA: Local Education Agency (school districts)

Limited English Proficiency (LEP): Refers to individuals whose dominant language is not English and who have difficulty speaking, reading, writing, or understanding the English language.

Motor Skills:

Fine motor: ability to use the hand in school activities, for example, writing and cutting.

Gross motor: ability to use arms and legs for activities like other children of their age.

M-team: A group of people who know the child or who may have done testing come together and try to come up with a plan to help make learning easier.

Multihandicapped: Children who have more than one handicap.

Native Language: The first language learned by the individual and/or used by the parents.

Non-English Speaking (NES): Students who do not speak English and would have difficulty in a regular English classroom.

Notice of the Determination: Formal paper sent to the parent telling them what program their child is in or what the special program they may have completed.

Occupational Therapy: Special help for children who need extra help with activities involving cutting, writing, drawing, tying, etc.

Orthopedically Handicapped (OH): Limits an individual's physical mobility and may interfere with school attendance or learning to such an extent that special services, training, materials, or facilities are required.

Override that revocation: When a school district does not accept a decision for a parent/guardian to refuse testing or placement.

Parent consultation: Information given by the parent.

Physical Therapy: Special help for children who need help with activities involving big muscles, i.e. jumping, catching, etc.

Placement: Program offered for the child to help make their learning easier.

Placement justification: Tells why the child needs a different approach to learning.

P.L. 94-142: Federal law which says it is the state's responsibility to educate all handicapped children (3-21 years). Known as "The Education for all Handicapped Children's Act of 1975".

Previous Interventions: Extra help the child has had before.

Prohibited: Forbidden or not allowed.

Re-evaluation: A student is tested every three years of sooner if there needs to be a change in their present program, i.e. dismissal, addition of more services/help.

Referred: To be tested to find ways to make learning easier.

Revoke: Take away or take back.

Silent period: A time in which language is learned by listening.

Special Education: Classes in which children who have been found to have EENs receive help from different programs or people depending on their needs. They may receive help in one or more of the following programs:

S/L: Speech-language
CD: Cognitively disabled
HI: Hearing impaired
LD: Learning disabled
ED: Emotionally disturbed

Specially Designed Physical Education: A special program for children not able to do activities in a regular gym class.

Speech-Language Program: Student has been evaluated and found to have difficulty learning their native language (understanding or using their language to communicate) which has been determined by an M-Team to interfere with their learning and/or social communication. The speech clinician helps children to understand or use the language necessary to be successful in the classroom or social situations.

Transitional Planning: Special planning for children to help them go to a higher level of education or a job.

Visually handicapped: Includes blind (total loss of vision or only minimal light perception), visually impaired (deviation in the structure or functioning of any part of parts of the eye), low vision (limitations in distance vision but may be able to see objects a few inches or feet away), visually limited (some visual limitations under some circumstances).

Hmong Glossary

Academic Achievement: Menyuam kawm tau zoo li cas hauv tsev kawm-ntawv

Adaptive Behavior: Kev koomtes thiab ua haujlwm tau nrog lwm tus

ADD/ADHD: Muaj teebmeem txog kam cuab pob-ntseg mloog

Advisor: Tus sablaj pab koj

Alternative M-team Report: Daim ntawv uas ib tug ntawm cov kws ntsuas xyuas (M-team) tsis pom zoo raws li lwm tus qhov kev tshawb pom

Assessment and Evaluation: Cov lus qhia txog ib tug menyuam kawm ntawv qhia los ntawm kev ntsuas xyuas

Autism: Ib qho kev muaj mob uas ua rau ib tus neeg tsis txawj hais lus los yog tham tsis tau rau lwm tus

Bilingual: Tus neeg txawj hais ob yam lus, tiam sis tsis tha hais ob yam lus zoo sib npauj

Bilingual Instruction: Kev cob-qhia rau cov menyuam tsis txawj lus Askiv zoo uas qhia ua lus Askiv thiab tus menyuam yam lus

Bilingualism: Kev ib tug menyuam kawm yam lus thib ob

    Additive: tom qab los yog ua ke thaum nws xyaum nws thawj yam lus

    Limited: Tus neeg hais tau ob yam lus, tabsis tsis tau kawm tag nrho ob yam ntawv

    Proficient: Tus neeg hais, nyeem, thiab sau tau ob yam lus zoo raws li thawj yam lus

    Subtractive: Kev tu ncua txog kev kawm thawj yam lus thiab kev tsis txawj los yog kev tsis nco qab thawj yam lus

Case Manager: Yog tus neeg uas, thaum ib tug menyuam raug xa mus kom muaj kev xeem ntsuas xyuas, nws hu cov neeg tuaj pab ntsuas xyuas, niam-txiv/tus saib xyuas, thiab sawvdaws txhua tus sib tham xyuas saib yam tug yuav pab tau tus menyuam

Classroom Observation: Tej yam uas pom nyob hauv chav kawm ntawv

Chapter 1: Qheb kev kawm uas kws qhia muab kev pab ntxiv paub txog kev nyeem ntawv thiab kev kawm leb (zauv)

Code Switching: Kev hloov ib yam lus rau lwm yam lub sijhawm tham lus

Cognitive: Peevxwm, kev ua tau

Cognitive Delay: Cov menyam uas kawm tau qeeb dua lawv cov phoojywg

Consent for Evaluation: Tso cai rau muaj kev ntsuas xyuas (xeem)

Decision Making Process: Kev txiav txim siab tias yuav ua licas

Delivery Model: Yuav muab kev pab licas nyob hauv chav kawm, lwm chav

Director or Designee: Tus neej saib xyuas cov ntaub ntawv thiab txiav txim siab tias yuav xa tus menyuam mus kawm licas

Discontinuation of Support Services: Qhov kawg ntawm kev pab vim tus menyuam tsis yuav qhov kev pab ntawd ntxiv lawm.

Due Process Hearing: Txoj kev lijchoj uas xyuas kom meej tias qhov kev pab rau tus menyuam ntawd txaus. Niam-txiv thiab tsev kawmntawv siv tau txoj cai no

Educational Outcome: Lub homphiaj uas koj xav tus menyuam mus txog

Emotionally Disturbed: Cov menyuam uas muaj teebmeem ua raws txoj cai uas ua rau muaj teebmeem kawm ntawv nyob hauv chav kawm

English as a Second Language: Kev qhia pab rau cov menyuam uas thawj yam lus tsis yog lus Askiv

Exceptional Educational Need: Cov menyuam uas muaj teebmeem kawm ntawv vim hais lus qeeb, tsis hnov lus, tsis mloog lus, kawm tsis tau, tes taw tsis muaj zog, hlwb tsis zoo

Fluent English Speaking: Paub lus Askiv txaus qhov yuav kawm tau nyob hauv chav cov paub lus Askiv kawm

Handicapping Condition: Xyuas ntawm qhov EEN

Hearing Impaired: Kev pab cov menyuam tsis hnov lus zoo tau txais kev pab ntxiv raws li saib lawv tsis hnov lus npaum licas

Hmong:
Hmong Leng/Green Hmong: Yog ib hom lus Hmoob ntsuab
White/Black Hmong: Yog ib hom lus Hmoob dawb/dub
Home Language: Yam lus hais hauv tsev uas tsis yog yam lus uas siv hais txog lwm yam nyob lwm qhov
Immunization: Tshuaj txhaj tiv thaiv kab mob
Individual Education Plan: Yog ib yam kev pab tsim tsa los ntawm ib pab neeg hais txog tus menyuam kev kawm, homphiaj raws xyoo, thiab kev xam pom xav yav tom ntej
I-94: Daim npav I-94 uas muab rau cov neeg thojnam lub sijhawm tuaj txog los yog rau cov neeg txawv tebchaws uas tau tuaj nyob hauv Asmeslikas tau ntev kom lawv muaj cai nyob raws kev lijchoj
Intervention Strategies: Cov kev qhia ntau yam uas muab los sim qhia saib menyuam kawm ntawv puas kawm tau
Language:
Conventional: Cov lus niaj hnub siv sib tham
Academic: Cov lus paub ua kom to taub thiab kawm tau ntawv
Language Dominance: Cov lus uas nws hais tau tsis daig
L1/First Language: Yam lus xub pib kawm tshaj plaws thaum pib xyaum hais lus
L2/Second Language: Yam lus thib ob uas yus kawm
Learning Disability (LD): Tus neeg muaj peevxwm ua tau yam ub yam no ib yam sawvdaws tabsis kawm tsis tau tej yam ntawv: xws li, (leb), nyeem ntawv, sau ntawv. Tus xibfwb qhia cov menyuam cim xeeb tsis zoo no pab kom cov menyuam no kawm tau
Limited English Proficiency (LEP): Hais txog cov tub neeg nws thawg lo tsis yog lus Askiv thiab nws muaj teeb meem hais lus, nyeem ntawv, thiab tsis to taub lus Askiv
Local Education Agency (LEA): Phab Kev Kawmntawv ntawm zej ntawm zos
Motor skills:
Fine motor: Kev Siv tes ua dej num hauv tsev kawm ntawv xws li yog sau ntawv, txiav ntawv
Gross motor: Kev siv tes-taw ua tau dej num raws li lwm dov menyuam muaj hnub nyoog ib yam
M-Team: Ib pab tub neeg paub los yog tau xeem tus menyuam koom tes ua kev los sib tham txog yuav muab kev pab li cas kom tus menyuam kawm tau ntawv yooj yim zog
Multi-handicapped: Hais txog cov menyuam uas xiam ob peb yam tes-taw
Native Language: Thawg yam lus uas ib tug neeg kawm los yog thawg yam lus niam-txiv siv
Non-English Speaking (NES): Hais txog cov menyuam tsis paub hais lus Askiv es muaj teeb meem kawm ntawv hauv chav uas siv lus Askiv
Notice of Determination: Daim ntawv xa rau niam-txiv qhia txog kev pab uas tus menyuam tab tom txais los yog kev pab phij-xej tus menyuam twb txais dhau los lawm
Occupational Therapy: Kev pab tshwj xeeb cov menyuam uas tes-taw tsis muaj zog ua dej num xws li txiav ntawv, sau ntawv, teeb duab, khi hlua, thiab lwm yam
Orthopedically Handicapped (OH): Hais txog cov tub neeg uas lub cev tsis muaj zog los yog txav tsis tshua tau es qhaj ntawv los yog muaj teeb meem kawm ntawv thiaj tau txais kev pab phij-xej los ntawm cov xibfwb, khoom pab thiab ntaub ntawv siv
Override that Revocation: Thaum tsev kawm ntawv log (School District) tsis pom zoo kev txiav txim los ntawm niam-txiv tsis pub tsev kawm ntawv xeem tus menyuam
Parent Consultation: Lus sablaj muab los ntawm niam-txiv
Pertaining: Hais txog
Physical Therapy: Kev pab tshwjxeeb pub rau cov menyuam uas yuav kev pab rau tej yam xws li: dhia los yog txhom tej yam dab tsi
Placement: Kev qhia muab pab rau tus menyuam kom nws txoj kev kawm yoojyim
Placement Justification: Kev qhia tias vim licas tus menyuam thiaj yuav txais lwm yam kev pab

114

PL 94-142: Txoj kev cai lijchoj Tseemfwv tebchaws uas qhia tias yog tseemfwv xeev haujlwm nrhiav kev pab rau cov menyuam puas hlob, tes, los yog taw (hnub nyoog 3-21 xyoos). Txoj cai no yog hu ua "The Education for All Handicapped Children Act of 1975."

Previous Interventions: Kev pub tshwjxeeb rau tus menyuam yav tas los

Prohibited: Tsis pub ua (Txwv tsis pub ua).

Re-evaluation: Kev xyuas saib cov menyuam cov kev pab yuav hloov licas, xws li: tshem lawv tawm ntawm qhov kev pab mus los yog ntxiv kev pab rau lawv

Referred: Kev ntsuas xyuas kom muaj kev pab ua kom kev kawm yoojyim ntxiv

Revoke: Txeeb mus los yog muab rov qab

Silent Period: Lub sijhawm kawm lus uas kom cov menyuam mloog

Special Education: Chav kawm uas muab pab rau cov menyuam uas pom tias yuav kev pab tshwjxeeb (EENs). Lawv yuav tau kawm ib nrab los yog tas cov kev kawm nram no los muaj:

    S/L: kawm hais lus

    CD: hais tsis tau lus

    HI: tsis hnov lus

    LD: cimxeeb tsis zoo (kawm tsis tau)

    ED: siab tsis tus (tswj tsis tau tus kheej)

Speically Designed Physical Education: Qhov kev pab rau cov menyuam uas koom tsis tau kev dhia tes-taw nrog cov tes-taw zoo

Speech and Language Program: Menyuam raug ntsuas pom tias kawm nws yam lus nyuaj. (totaub los yog siv nws yam lus sib tham nyuaj) uas cov kws ntsuam xyuas pom tau tias yuav muaj teebmeem rau nws txoj kev hais lus. Tus kws qhia hais lus totaub thiab siv kev pab kom tus menyuam kawm tau lus thiab hais tau lus nrog neeg

Transitional Planning: Kev sablaj npaj rau menyuam kom pab lawv nce mus rau qib kawm siab zog los yog npaj rau kev haujlwm

Traumatic Brain Injury: Tus neeg uas ua raug nws lub taubhau ua rau puas hlwb uas yuavtsum nrhiav kev pab los qhia

Visually Handicapped: Hais txog cov dig muag (cov tsis pom kev hlo li los yog tsis tshua pom kev xwb los yog), qhov muag puas (qhov muag txawv men tsis), tsis pom kev deb (tsis pom deb, tabsis tseem pom ze ze, tsis pom kev zoo (tsis pom zoo rau tej lub sijhawm)

LEP Levels of English as a Second Language Students

The Department of Public Instruction requires that limited-English proficient (LEP) students be assigned a number from 1 to 6 to indicate their proficiency level. These numbers in no way correspond to the grade or class level. Advancement from one LEP level to another is not a function of time. A stu.dent may remain at one level for a number of years.

Level 1: No English

Students are at the very beginning of learning English. Except for a word here or there, students are able to understand little or no English. They may be able to imitate words and phrases.

	English	Hmong
Does the child understand only minimal English orHmong?	Yes No	Yes No
Does the student imitate words and phrases?	Yes No	Yes No

Level 2: Receptive English only

Students are able to understand conversational English in varying degrees. They can produce some common English words and phrases spontaneously and repeat short sentences or questions, but they are unable to use English to communicate their thoughts and opinions.

	English	Hmong
Does the student understand informal conversational English or Hmong?	Yes No	Yes No
Does the student produce common English or Hmong words and phrases spontaneously?	Yes No	Yes No
Does the student repeat short sentences or questions?	Yes No	Yes No
Does the student express thoughts and opinions primarily in Hmong?	Yes No	Yes No

Level 3: Survival English

In speaking, these students sometimes omit nouns or verbs and make many errors in the use of articles, pronouns, and verb endings. These students are usually able to communicate ideas and feelings in English, but with difficulty, due to limited vocabulary. They understand parts of lessons and follow very simple directions.

Does the student sometimes omit nouns or verbs?	Yes	No
Does the student err in use of articles, pronouns, or verb endings?	Yes	No
Does the student express ideas and feelings in English but with difficulty due to limited vocabulary?	Yes	No
Does the student understand parts of lessons?	Yes	No
Does the student follow very simple directions?	Yes	No

Student has been at this level for

Level 4: Intermediate English

Students understand, speak, read, and write English with some degree of hesitancy. They usually control syntactic structures that include some plurals, articles, pronouns, and verb endings. Complex verb forms are often confused. There is more variation of proficiency within Level 4 than within other levels. Students may remain at this level a long time.

Does the student understand, speak, read, and write English with some degree of hesitancy?	Yes	No
Does the student use syntactic structures using some plurals articles, pronouns, and verb endings?	Yes	No
Does the student confuse complex verb forms?	Yes	No

Student has been at this level for

Level 5: Nearly Proficient English

Students demonstrate a fairly high degree of proficiency in understanding and speaking English. They control most of the basic grammatical structures of English. For older students, this level represents incomplete learning of some of the more advanced structures. They still require assistance because achievement may not be a level appropriate for their age or grade.

Does the student demonstrate a fairly high degree of proficiency in understanding English?	Yes	No
Does the student demonstrate a fairly high degree of speaking English?	Yes	No
Does the student use most of the basic grammatical structures of English?	Yes	No
Does the student require English as a Second Language assistance because achievement is not at a level appropriate for his or her grade level?	Yes	No

Level 6: Proficient English

Students understand, speak, read, and write English proficiently and no longer qualify for any English as a Second Language assistance.

Does the student understand, speak, read, and write English proficiently and no longer qualify for English as a Second Language assistance?	Yes	No